FOCUS

THE 30-DAY TRANSFORMATION

LOKENDER SHARMA

AF651752

BlueRose ONE .com
Stories Matter
NewDelhi • London

BLUEROSE PUBLISHERS
India | U.K.

Copyright © Lokender Sharma 2025

All rights reserved by author. No part of this publication may be reproduced, stored in a retrieval system or transmitted in any form or by any means, electronic, mechanical, photocopying, recording or otherwise, without the prior permission of the author. Although every precaution has been taken to verify the accuracy of the information contained herein, the publisher assumes no responsibility for any errors or omissions. No liability is assumed for damages that may result from the use of information contained within.

BlueRose Publishers takes no responsibility for any damages, losses, or liabilities that may arise from the use or misuse of the information, products, or services provided in this publication.

For permissions requests or inquiries regarding this publication, please contact:

BLUEROSE PUBLISHERS
www.BlueRoseONE.com
info@bluerosepublishers.com
+91 8882 898 898
+4407342408967

ISBN: 978-93-7139-365-2

Cover Design: Shubham Verma
Typesetting: Sagar

First Edition: July 2025

Dedication

To my beloved parents,

This book is dedicated to you — the ones who have shaped me, inspired me, and taught me the true meaning of perseverance, focus, and unconditional love. Your sacrifices, guidance, and unwavering belief in me have laid the foundation for everything I do.

May this work be a small reflection of the values you instilled in me, and may it inspire others the way you have always inspired me.

With all my love and gratitude,

-Lokender Sharma

Preface

In today's world, we are surrounded by distractions — the constant ping of notifications, the lure of social media, the endless scroll of entertainment, and the pressure to multitask. It's no wonder that many of us struggle to focus, to stay present, and to give our best effort to what truly matters. We are constantly battling against a stream of external stimuli that chips away at our attention, leaving us feeling drained, overwhelmed, and unproductive.

But what if I told you that the real enemy isn't the technology, the noise, or the distractions? The real enemy is **how we choose to react** to them. The true challenge lies not in the world around us but in mastering **our internal world** — our ability to direct our attention, to create empowering habits, and to cultivate a mindset that aligns with our deepest desires and goals.

This book, **Focus 30**, is a guide to taking back control of your attention. Over the next 30 days, we will embark on a journey of self-discovery, reset, and transformation. Each week focuses on building habits that foster deep concentration, unwavering commitment, and the mental clarity needed to achieve extraordinary results.

The first week is all about **Awareness and Reset** — understanding how distractions work, identifying the habits that sabotage our focus, and establishing a new foundation for success. Week two will help you **install new focus habits** that become second nature, from mastering time management to setting up your environment for peak productivity. In the third week, we'll dive deep into **Mind Mastery**, teaching you how to control your thoughts, delay gratification, and clear the mental clutter that holds you back. Finally, in week four, you'll learn how to make **Focus a Lifelong Practice**, integrating these principles into your daily routine for sustained success.

As you turn the pages of this book, know that this isn't just another productivity guide. This is a roadmap to a life where you are fully in control of your time, your attention, and your future. The methods you'll discover here aren't about quick fixes or shortcuts — they are about building a sustainable, intentional way of living that serves your highest potential.

In this journey, there will be moments of challenge and discomfort, but there will also be moments of profound clarity and growth. **True transformation begins the moment you decide to take full responsibility for your focus** — and that is exactly what you are about to do.

How to Use This Book

To make the most out of this book, approach it with full commitment. Each week will guide you through different concepts and actionable steps. Take your time to reflect, experiment, and implement the practices before moving on. The exercises and activities at the end of each week are designed to solidify what you've learned. Do not rush through them. The goal is not just to read but to **apply**. Consider journaling your thoughts, tracking your progress, and revisiting sections whenever you feel challenged or off-track. Most importantly, remember — consistency over time is the key to lasting change.

Are you ready to reclaim your focus, reset your mind, and unlock a future of limitless possibilities?

Let's begin.

- Lokender Sharma

Contents

CHAPTER 1

The Real Enemy: Distraction

You woke up this morning, full of potential. The day was fresh, and so was your mind, ready to take on challenges, learn something new, and make progress. But as the minutes ticked by, something happened. Something that you didn't even realize was happening.

Your phone buzzed. You picked it up without thinking. "Just one quick check," you told yourself. But you know how it goes. One check turns into another, and before you realize it, an hour has passed. You had intended to study, work on a project, or maybe just plan your day, but instead, your focus had drifted. A series of notifications, a scroll through social media, a video on YouTube – everything was calling your name, each moment a little louder, each distraction a little harder to ignore.

What happened? Why is it so easy to give in to these distractions? Why do they always seem to pull you away from what you really want to achieve?

The answer is simple, yet profound: Distraction is not something outside of you. The real enemy is inside. It's not the phone, or social media, or even the people around you. It's your mind, caught in a loop of seeking instant gratification. It's the ease with which you can avoid something uncomfortable, the way you flee from tasks that require focus, and the comfort of putting off responsibility for another moment.

You've experienced it countless times. You sit down to study, but suddenly you feel bored, restless. Your mind starts to wander. You think about something else, anything else, to fill the gap. And so, you open Instagram or start watching a video. It's an escape. A way to avoid the discomfort of the task at hand. But in doing so, you are not just avoiding work; you're training your brain to fear effort. You're telling yourself that it's okay to avoid challenges, that it's easier to give in to distractions. The more you give in, the more your brain gets comfortable with avoidance. And that, in turn, makes focusing harder every time.

But today, everything changes. You've just stepped into Focus 30 – a 30-day journey to break free from distractions and reclaim your power over your focus. This is the first step in a long process of transformation.

For the next 30 days, your task isn't to blame your phone or social media. It's not about getting rid of distractions completely – that's impossible. Instead, it's about becoming aware. It's about taking responsibility for where your attention is going. It's about recognizing when your mind starts to wander and making the choice to pull it back in, to refocus on what matters.

Distraction is not your enemy. The enemy is the lack of awareness. Every time you get distracted, it's a sign that you weren't paying attention to what truly matters. But by simply becoming aware of your distractions, you take the first step toward mastery. You take control of your mind. You regain the power to focus.

So, here's what we are going to do today: You are going to start by becoming aware of your distractions. No, we're not going to try to eliminate them yet. First, we need to understand them. We need to observe them, recognize them, and start questioning why we give in to them.

Your task for today is simple, but powerful. Take a few minutes, grab a journal or your Focus Tracker, and **answer these three questions:**

1. What are the 3 biggest distractions that steal my time every day?
2. At what time of day do I find myself getting distracted the most?
3. How would my life feel if I removed these distractions for 30 days?

Don't rush through this. Take your time. Think about how each distraction pulls you away from your goals. Reflect on how much time is lost and what it's costing you in terms of progress, learning, and personal growth.

By becoming aware of these distractions, you are already taking the first step toward regaining control. You're setting the foundation for a new habit: one where you choose focus over avoidance, where you actively work to train your brain to embrace effort rather than escape it.

Remember, distraction is not your enemy. The real enemy is your lack of awareness. And today, we begin the process of transforming that awareness into action.

Welcome to Focus 30. Over the next 30 days, you will develop the power to focus like never before. This journey is going to change everything. And it starts today.

Task Recap:

1. Write down your top 3 distractions.
2. Identify the time of day when you're most distracted.
3. Reflect on how you would feel if you removed these distractions for 30 days.

CHAPTER 2
Your Focus Score

Yesterday, we took the first step in understanding distraction. Today, we'll turn the lens inward. It's time to assess your focus – to measure where you stand right now, so that we can track your improvement over the next 30 days. Without measuring, there can be no progress. Without knowing where you are, it's impossible to know where you need to go.

It's easy to assume that you know how focused you are. Maybe you think, "I can focus when I really try," or "I can do it, I just get distracted sometimes." But the truth is, we often underestimate how much our focus wavers, and how often distractions subtly derail our best intentions.

In fact, a lot of us spend much of the day *reacting* to things around us – phone notifications, emails, conversations, and other people's demands. But focusing, true focus, is about becoming proactive. It's about choosing to direct your attention toward what matters most, and staying on course, even when the distractions are pulling at you.

So, how do we measure that? How do we figure out where you really stand?

The answer is simple: You take a Focus Assessment.

Today, we'll work through a 10-question Focus Assessment designed to give you a snapshot of your current focus levels. The answers you give will not define you forever, but they'll give us a baseline – a starting point. From here, we'll track your improvement over the next 30 days, and see just how far you can go.

Let's dive into the Focus Assessment.

Focus Assessment:

Take a moment to answer the following 10 questions honestly. These questions are designed to measure how often you feel distracted, how easily you lose focus, and how you react to challenges. Your answers will help us understand where you're starting from.

1. How often do you find yourself checking your phone or social media when you should be focusing on something else?

- Never
- Rarely
- Sometimes
- Often
- Almost Always

2. How often do you feel restless or bored when trying to focus on a task for more than 10 minutes?

- Never
- Rarely
- Sometimes
- Often
- Almost Always

3. When you face a difficult task, how often do you find yourself looking for something easier to do?

- Never
- Rarely
- Sometimes
- Often
- Almost Always

4. How often do you get distracted by something unexpected, like a new notification or a phone call, while you're in the middle of a task?

- Never
- Rarely
- Sometimes
- Often
- Almost Always

5. How often do you find it hard to stay focused on a single task for more than 30 minutes at a time?

- Never
- Rarely
- Sometimes
- Often
- Almost Always

6. When you're working on a project, how often do you jump between tasks without finishing any one of them?

- Never
- Rarely
- Sometimes
- Often
- Almost Always

7. How often do you feel overwhelmed by the number of things you need to focus on at once?

- Never
- Rarely
- Sometimes
- Often
- Almost Always

8. How frequently do you lose track of time when you're supposed to be working or studying?

- Never
- Rarely
- Sometimes
- Often
- Almost Always

9. When you're working, how often do you find yourself thinking about other things unrelated to your task?

- Never
- Rarely
- Sometimes
- Often
- Almost Always

10. How often do you struggle to get started on important tasks or projects?

- Never
- Rarely
- Sometimes
- Often
- Almost Always

How to Evaluate Your Focus Score:

Now, take a moment to count up your answers. Each time you selected "Never," give yourself 1 point. For "Rarely," give yourself 2 points. For "Sometimes," give yourself 3 points. For "Often," give yourself 4 points. And for "Almost Always," give yourself 5 points.

Once you've added up your total, you'll have your Focus Score.

Focus Score Breakdown:

- ***10-20 Points:*** *You are highly focused, and distractions are not significantly affecting your ability to stay on task. You have a strong sense of discipline and control over your attention. You're well on your way to mastering your focus.*
- ***21-30 Points:*** *You have a fair amount of focus, but distractions occasionally get the best of you. There's room for improvement. You might find yourself slipping into distractions now and then, but you have the potential to sharpen your focus.*
- ***31-40 Points:*** *Focus is a struggle for you. Distractions tend to pull you away from your tasks more often than not. You often find it difficult to concentrate for long periods. The good news is that you've just identified this challenge, and over the next 30 days, we'll work on improving this significantly.*
- ***41-50 Points:*** *Your focus is deeply compromised by distractions. You find it extremely difficult to stay on task and regularly get sidetracked. But don't worry — recognizing where you are is the first step to improvement.*

This is the perfect time for a reset, and with consistent effort, you'll notice real changes.

What Now?

Now that you have your Focus Score, it's time to reflect. Take a moment to think about the questions that stood out to you the most. Which ones felt most difficult to answer? Which distractions are the hardest to resist? This is your starting point.

You've just taken the first step in the Focus 30 challenge. Now, it's all about progress. Over the next 30 days, we'll help you strengthen your focus, one day at a time. And every time you take this test again; you'll see how much improvement you've made.

Remember, this isn't about being perfect. It's about being aware and constantly improving. Let's see how much you can grow over the next 30 days.

Task Recap:

1. Complete the Focus Assessment.
2. Review your Focus Score and reflect on the areas where you need improvement.
3. Commit to improving your focus every day, starting with small actions.

CHAPTER 3

Apps That Are Killing You

It's easy to dismiss them as harmless – those apps on your phone that keep you entertained for hours. "SnapFeed," "ShortFlix," or "BattleForce"—apps that seem to make the day fly by. We convince ourselves that they're just small distractions, a little "break" in between tasks. But let me ask you something: How often does that break turn into hours of lost time? How many times have you sat down to get something done, only to find yourself scrolling endlessly, or battling it out in a mobile game that you never really planned to play in the first place?

Today, we're going to take a hard look at three of the most popular apps that are killing your productivity. I'm not here to judge you for using them. Heck, I've been there too. These apps aren't inherently bad – they serve a purpose. But when used mindlessly, they become silent killers of focus, energy, and time. If you've ever felt like your phone was controlling you rather than the other way around, you know exactly what I'm talking about.

Today, we're going to talk about SnapFeed, ShortFlix, and BattleForce – and you're going to make a choice. A choice that can change your productivity, your focus, and ultimately, your life.

SnapFeed: The Endless Scroll

SnapFeed, the popular visual storytelling app, is one of the most addictive social media platforms worldwide. It's designed to grab your attention, keep you hooked, and make you feel like you're always connected to the latest trends, updates, and events. And here's the thing – SnapFeed is built on algorithms that make sure the content you see is tailor-made to keep you engaged. It's not just random images and posts; it's a flood of things that you like, that you care about, that make you feel good – but also, things that are utterly distracting.

How many times have you told yourself, "I'll just check SnapFeed for five minutes"? And then, before you know it, an hour has passed, and you've gone down a rabbit hole of posts, stories, and reels. The infinite scroll makes it so easy to keep going. It's designed to never stop – to keep you coming back for more.

But here's the thing: That hour you just spent scrolling, did it bring you closer to your goals? Did it move you forward in any way? Or did it just keep you in a loop, a temporary distraction that you'll have to shake off to get back on track?

SnapFeed is great for keeping up with friends and trends, but if you let it, it can steal more of your time than you realize. The truth is, it thrives on your distraction. Every second you spend on SnapFeed is a second taken away from your real life, your dreams, and your focus.

ShortFlix: The 60-Second Trap

ShortFlix has become the new sensation in the world of entertainment. The platform delivers bite-sized, 60-second videos that are easy to consume, whether you're looking for something funny, motivational, or informative. ShortFlix has everything that can keep you hooked. Quick, punchy content that demands little time but offers huge rewards in terms of entertainment. Sounds harmless, right?

But here's the catch: those 60 seconds are designed to pull you into the next video, and the next, and the next. Before you know it, you've watched 30 minutes of random videos. You start out with a goal, maybe you just want to check a short clip about something you're interested in, and suddenly, you're in an endless loop. One video turns into ten, and now you've wasted your entire evening.

ShortFlix isn't just a platform for quick entertainment—it's a well-crafted distraction that trains your brain to need constant stimulation. Think about it. Your brain begins to crave this short-term pleasure, this quick fix of dopamine. It teaches you that long, focused work is not as rewarding as the instant gratification of jumping from one video to the next.

The problem isn't the content on ShortFlix itself. The problem is the behaviour it fosters. It teaches you to get bored quickly, to feel like anything that takes longer than a minute isn't worth your attention. And that's the exact opposite of what you need when it comes to building focus and discipline.

BattleForce: The Battle for Your Time

BattleForce, a mobile game that has gained massive popularity, is the ultimate test of your attention span. It's fast-paced, competitive, and immersive. Whether you're playing solo, in teams, or competing in a tournament, it can be exhilarating. The thrill of battling opponents, the strategy, and the excitement of leveling up – BattleForce has everything that keeps you glued to your screen.

But here's the problem: gaming, especially games like BattleForce, has a way of stealing your focus without you even realizing it. A quick match here and there turns into a few hours spent in the game. You might tell yourself, "I'll just play one match," but one match often turns into five, then ten, and before you know it, your entire day has disappeared.

The issue with BattleForce isn't that it's a bad game—it's that it's designed to keep you playing. You're constantly working to improve, to win, to level up. The game rewards your time and attention with small, satisfying wins. But here's the catch: those wins are temporary. They give you a rush, but they don't move you closer to your bigger goals in life. How many hours have you spent in the game that you could have used to improve your skills, learn something new, or advance in your studies?

Every minute you spend playing BattleForce is a minute you've chosen to invest in something that ultimately doesn't contribute to your growth. Gaming can be fun, but if it's taking over your life and distracting you from what truly matters, it becomes a silent thief of time.

Your Decision: Uninstall or Pause

Now that we've taken a close look at the apps that are potentially stealing your time, here's the big decision: Uninstall or Pause the apps that are killing your focus.

Today, we're asking you to take action. Choose three apps that distract you the most. Maybe it's SnapFeed, ShortFlix, BattleForce, or any other app that keeps you from staying focused. Now, decide: Are you going to uninstall them for the next 30 days, or are you going to pause your use for a while?

Don't worry, this isn't permanent. You can always reinstall them later if you feel like it, but for the next 30 days, we want you to take a break from them. This detox is not about cutting off from the world. It's about taking control of your time and energy.

Here's what you need to do today:

- Uninstall or Pause the top 3 most distracting apps on your phone.
- Reflect on how you feel. Do you feel liberated, or do you feel like you've lost something important?
- Write down your thoughts in your journal or Focus Tracker. How do you think your focus will improve without these distractions?

Task Recap:

1. Identify your top 3 distracting apps.
2. Uninstall or Pause them for the next 30 days.

3. Reflect on how these apps have been affecting your focus and how you feel without them.

By eliminating the apps that distract you, you're taking the first step toward building stronger focus. This isn't just about detoxing for a month – it's about realizing how much control these apps have over your time and making the conscious decision to take that control back.

CHAPTER 4
Dopamine Detox Explained

In today's digital age, we are surrounded by constant distractions. Our phones, social media, games, and even advertisements are designed to capture our attention. These distractions constantly trigger our brain's reward system, specifically the release of a chemical called dopamine, which gives us feelings of pleasure and satisfaction.

While dopamine is a necessary chemical in our brain for motivation and learning, the problem arises when we become addicted to these dopamine hits, particularly in the form of instant gratification. The more dopamine we get from quick, easy rewards—like checking social media notifications or playing mobile games—the harder it becomes to focus on tasks that require sustained attention and effort.

This is where the concept of a "**dopamine detox**" comes in. A dopamine detox is essentially a reset for your brain. It involves stepping away from all sources of instant gratification—like your phone, social media, entertainment, and other distractions—for a designated period. The goal? To break the cycle of constant stimulation and reprogram your brain to regain control over your attention and focus.

Why Dopamine Detox is Essential

Think of your brain like a muscle. Just like how you would train your body for physical endurance, you need to train your brain for focus and concentration. When you continuously give in to distractions, your brain's reward system gets hijacked, making it more difficult to focus on tasks that require more time and effort.

Over time, this constant bombardment of stimuli results in reduced attention spans, poorer concentration, and increased levels of stress and anxiety. Your brain becomes used to the quick dopamine hits, and anything that doesn't offer immediate gratification feels boring or difficult.

This phenomenon has a significant impact on how you study, work, and even interact with the world. Tasks that once required focus—like reading a book, completing an assignment, or even having a conversation—become harder because your brain is overstimulated and is constantly craving the next quick fix.

A dopamine detox is essentially a reset. By cutting off access to sources of instant gratification for a certain period, you allow your brain to recalibrate itself. This can help you regain control over your attention, rewire your focus, and help you get back to doing deep, meaningful work.

How Dopamine Detox Works

A dopamine detox is not about eliminating all pleasurable experiences from your life. Instead, it's about limiting the overuse of things that cause an artificial dopamine spike—things like social media, video games, excessive internet browsing, and even binge-watching TV shows. These things, although fun and entertaining, provide little to no long-term satisfaction or personal growth.

When you stop exposing yourself to these constant sources of dopamine, your brain slowly starts to recover. You begin to regain control over your impulses, your attention span improves, and your capacity for deep focus grows. This detox allows your brain to return to its natural state of engagement with the world, without being constantly distracted by fleeting sources of pleasure.

The detox works in several ways:

- Restores Focus and Clarity: By taking a break from instant gratification, you allow your brain to settle into a more focused, calm, and clear state. This leads to a greater ability to concentrate on tasks that require time and effort.
- Boosts Long-Term Satisfaction: When you stop seeking instant gratification, you begin to enjoy the process of working toward longer-term rewards. Tasks that once felt tedious or boring now become more engaging because your brain is no longer preoccupied with seeking dopamine.
- Reduces Stress and Anxiety: Constant exposure to dopamine-driven activities, like checking your phone or social media, can lead to a rise in stress and anxiety levels. A dopamine detox can help alleviate this by reducing the constant need for external stimulation and allowing you to experience a sense of calm.

The Science Behind Dopamine Detox

Dopamine is a neurotransmitter in the brain that plays a role in motivation, pleasure, and learning. It is released when you experience something rewarding, such as eating your favourite food, getting a like on your social media post, or winning a game. While dopamine is important for survival (it encourages us to repeat behaviours that benefit us), its overuse in today's digital age has led to addiction-like behaviour.

When you get a dopamine hit, your brain feels pleasure. But over time, as you become used to these quick rewards, your brain starts to require more intense stimuli to produce the same level of satisfaction. This is why the continuous use of apps like Instagram or the addiction to mobile gaming can make you feel increasingly restless and unable to focus on more important tasks. The brain essentially becomes desensitized to normal levels of pleasure, causing you to seek more immediate and intense stimulation.

A dopamine detox helps reset this system. By reducing or eliminating access to dopamine-releasing activities, you lower your brain's threshold for stimulation. You allow your dopamine receptors to "reset" so that you can once again enjoy the process of completing meaningful, focused tasks without the need for constant external rewards.

Implementing Your Dopamine Detox

Here's the simple approach for implementing a dopamine detox in your life:

- **Start Small:** You don't have to do a full-on detox for weeks or months. Start by setting a specific period of time—12 hours, for example—where you eliminate all forms of entertainment content. This means no social media, no YouTube, no Netflix, no games. You can still use your phone for work, communication, or emergencies, but the focus should be on cutting out sources of mindless entertainment.

- **Identify Your Triggers:** Before starting your detox, identify the things that trigger your need for dopamine. Is it the moment you wake up and grab your phone? Is it the habit of checking social media when you feel bored? These triggers are the starting point for breaking your dependence on instant gratification.
- **Replace with Productive Activities:** Instead of mindlessly scrolling through your phone, use the detox time for activities that improve your well-being, like reading, meditating, going for a walk, or working on a project that requires deep focus. These activities help restore your attention and improve your long-term satisfaction.
- **Gradual Reintegration:** After completing the detox, don't immediately dive back into old habits. Gradually reintroduce entertainment or social media, but do so with awareness. Set boundaries. For example, limit social media usage to 30 minutes a day, or designate specific times for watching TV or playing games.

The Benefits of Dopamine Detox

The benefits of a dopamine detox are numerous. Here are just a few of the most significant ones:

- **Improved Focus and Productivity:** Once your brain has recalibrated, you'll notice an improvement in your ability to focus. Tasks that previously seemed overwhelming will feel more manageable. You'll be able to sit down and work for longer periods without feeling the urge to check your phone or do something more stimulating.

- **Increased Self-Control:** By taking control of your dopamine levels, you'll improve your self-discipline. You'll no longer be at the mercy of distractions and your own cravings for instant gratification. Instead, you'll regain the power to direct your attention where it's most needed.
- **Enhanced Mental Clarity:** With less mental clutter from constant distractions, you'll experience clearer thinking and better decision-making. Your mind will feel more at peace, and you'll become better at handling tasks that require deep thought.
- **Greater Long-Term Satisfaction:** By reducing your dependence on short-term dopamine hits, you'll begin to derive greater satisfaction from long-term achievements. Whether it's completing a project, learning a new skill, or cultivating a meaningful relationship, you'll find more joy in the process rather than seeking instant rewards.

Your Challenge: 12-Hour Dopamine Detox

Today's challenge is simple: eliminate all entertainment content for 12 hours. This includes social media, games, movies, TV shows, or anything that gives you an instant dopamine boost.

This may feel uncomfortable at first, and it's okay if it's challenging. The goal is not perfection, but to make progress toward regaining control over your attention. By cutting out these distractions for a few hours, you're giving your brain the space to recalibrate.

The next time you feel the urge to check your phone or jump into a game, take a deep breath. Remember that your focus is a muscle, and today, you're training it to become stronger. After 12 hours, reflect on how you feel—do you feel more focused? More peaceful? More in control?

CHAPTER 5
Phone Rules Setup

We live in an era where our phones are no longer just tools for communication—they've become integral to every part of our lives. From social media to work emails, news updates to entertainment, our phones seem to demand our attention at every moment. While smartphones are incredibly useful, their constant presence in our lives also makes them a significant source of distraction.

The reality is that smartphones are designed to capture your attention. Notifications, vibrations, sounds—they are all strategically engineered to make you check your phone again and again. This constant cycle of checking and rechecking can seriously interfere with your focus and productivity. But the good news is, you don't need to quit your phone entirely. You just need to regain control over it. This is where phone rules come in.

In this chapter, we'll discuss how to set up rules for using your phone effectively so that it serves you instead of distracting you. These rules will help you regain control of your time, enhance your productivity, and ensure that your phone is a tool for success, not a source of endless distraction.

Why You Need Phone Rules

Without any boundaries, your phone can easily become a time-sucking machine. Whether it's mindlessly scrolling through social media, getting lost in an endless stream of videos, or simply checking notifications every few minutes, these behaviours create a constant drain on your attention and energy.

The average person spends several hours a day on their phone. According to reports, the average screen time in a day is around 3 to 4 hours, and many people check their phone 200 to 300 times a day. That's a lot of time spent distracted, away from productive tasks. The constant engagement with your phone pulls your attention away from tasks that require deep focus and long-term effort, like studying, working, or even having meaningful conversations.

By setting phone rules, you create clear boundaries that allow you to use your phone as a tool, rather than allowing it to control your life. When you have control over your phone, you can decide when and how to engage with it, instead of letting it dictate your actions. This chapter will guide you through the process of setting rules that will empower you to take back control of your time and focus.

The Essential Phone Rules You Need

1. No Phone in Bed

The first and perhaps most important rule is to keep your phone out of your bed. This might seem small, but it has a massive impact on your productivity, mental clarity, and sleep quality. When you bring your phone into your bed, you're inviting distractions into your space of rest. You may end up scrolling through social media or checking emails long after you've intended to fall asleep. Not only does this reduce your quality of sleep, but it also disrupts your ability to unwind and relax before bed.

Why this rule works:

- **Improves sleep quality:** Avoiding screens before bed can help you fall asleep faster and enjoy a deeper, more restful sleep. The blue light emitted by screens interferes with the production of melatonin, the hormone responsible for regulating sleep.
- **Prevents mindless scrolling:** When you keep your phone out of the bed, you prevent yourself from engaging in late-night mindless scrolling, which often leads to wasted time and added stress.

How to implement it:

- Place your phone on a nearby table, dresser, or charging station—anywhere that's not within arm's reach.
- Consider using an alarm clock instead of relying on your phone to wake you up in the morning. This way, you won't be tempted to start scrolling as soon as you wake up.

2. Fixed Usage Time

It's easy to lose track of time when you're using your phone. Whether it's checking messages, browsing social media, or watching videos, the minutes turn into hours without you realizing it. That's why setting fixed usage times is crucial. This rule is all about establishing clear time limits for how long you spend on your phone throughout the day.

Why this rule works:

- **Prevents time wastage:** By allocating specific time slots for phone usage, you ensure that you don't spend excessive time on your device.
- **Boosts focus:** When you know that you have a set time to check your phone, you can focus on other tasks without the constant urge to check your screen.

How to implement it:

- Set specific time blocks during which you can use your phone. For example, allow yourself 30 minutes of social media use after lunch or set 15-minute check-ins every few hours to catch up on messages.
- Use a timer or alarm to signal the end of your phone time so you don't get carried away.
- To take it further, you can use apps that block or limit access to social media and other distracting apps during your fixed working hours.

3. No Phone During Study or Work Time

This is one of the most effective rules for maintaining focus and productivity. Phones are the biggest disruptor when it comes to deep work. A single notification or the urge to check your phone can break your concentration and make it harder to get back into the task at hand.

Why this rule works:

- Increases productivity: By completely removing the temptation of checking your phone, you give your brain the chance to focus deeply on the task at hand.

- Reduces distractions: Every time you check your phone, you interrupt your thought process. This constant switching between tasks makes it harder for your brain to stay focused and perform at its best.

How to implement it:

- Keep your phone in another room or at least out of your immediate reach when studying or working. If you use your phone for work-related tasks, make sure to set clear boundaries, such as only checking your emails during specific times.
- Use apps that block access to distracting apps during study or work hours. Alternatively, you can enable "Do Not Disturb" mode to silence incoming notifications during your designated focus times.

4. Uninstall or Mute Non-Essential Notifications

One of the main sources of distraction on your phone is notifications. These alerts constantly pull you away from your work or personal time, making it nearly impossible to stay focused. To regain control over your phone, consider uninstalling apps that are not essential or muting their notifications altogether.

Why this rule works:

- Minimizes distractions: By removing notifications, you limit the number of times you're interrupted throughout the day.
- Reduces anxiety: Constant notifications can trigger feelings of urgency and stress, even if they're not important. By eliminating these distractions, you reduce unnecessary anxiety.

How to implement it:

- Go through your apps and identify those that are not essential to your daily life. Uninstall or at least mute notifications for these apps.
- Set up notification preferences on your phone so that you only get alerts for important messages, calls, or updates.

5. Screen-Free Meals and Social Time

In many households, it's common to check your phone during meals or when spending time with family and friends. However, this is not ideal. Meals and social gatherings are opportunities to connect with the people around you, and phones often distract us from these valuable moments.

Why this rule works:

- **Fosters real connections:** By putting your phone away, you can engage more meaningfully with those around you.
- **Improves mindfulness:** Eating without distractions helps you be more mindful of your food, improving digestion and enhancing the enjoyment of your meal.

How to implement it:

- Make it a rule to leave your phone in another room during meals or social interactions. If you're dining out or spending time with friends, focus on the present moment instead of your phone.
- Use a phone box or a designated space where everyone places their phones when eating together.

How to Stick to Your Phone Rules

Setting these phone rules is a great first step, but the real challenge lies in sticking to them. Here are a few strategies to help you stay disciplined:

- **Set reminders:** Use your calendar or reminders app to set alerts for when it's time to stop using your phone.
- **Track screen time:** Most smartphones now come with screen time tracking features. Regularly check how much time you spend on your phone and compare it to your goals.
- **Accountability partner:** Share your phone rules with a friend or family member who can help keep you accountable.

Conclusion

By setting clear and intentional rules for phone usage, you're taking control of one of the biggest distractions in modern life. These rules allow you to use your phone as a tool to enhance your productivity, rather than letting it dictate how you spend your time. With these boundaries in place, you can cultivate healthier habits, improve your focus, and make your phone work for you rather than against you.

CHAPTER 6
Trigger–Routine–Reward Loop

You're sitting at your desk, ready to work, but as soon as you hear your phone buzz or see a notification pop up, you find yourself reaching for your device. Minutes later, you're scrolling through social media or watching a video, completely distracted from the task at hand. You may even feel a sense of relief or pleasure when you check your phone. This loop of distraction is a powerful mechanism in the brain that's constantly working against your focus and productivity. But understanding this cycle can help you break it and regain control over your time.

In this chapter, we'll dive deep into the "Trigger–Routine–Reward" loop that governs our distractions and show you how to disrupt it so that you can reclaim your attention.

The Science Behind the Loop

At its core, the Trigger–Routine–Reward loop is based on a principle known as operant conditioning, which was first introduced by psychologist B.F. Skinner. The cycle involves three key components:

- **Trigger:** This is the initial cue that prompts you to start a certain behaviour. It could be something external like a notification, a sound, or even an internal feeling such as boredom or anxiety.
- **Routine:** Once triggered, you automatically engage in a certain behaviour. This could be anything from checking your phone, scrolling through Instagram, or even getting up to grab a snack. The routine is a habit that has formed over time, often as a response to the trigger.
- **Reward:** After completing the routine, you experience a reward, whether it's the satisfaction of seeing a new message or the short-term pleasure of watching a funny video. This reward reinforces the behaviour, making it more likely that you'll repeat the cycle the next time the trigger occurs.

When this loop is reinforced over and over, it becomes ingrained in your brain, making it harder to break free. Every time you respond to a trigger with a routine and a reward, your brain creates stronger connections between these components, forming a habit.

How the Loop Works in Your Life

Let's break down how this loop plays out in your everyday routine:

- **Trigger:** You're working on a task, and suddenly, you hear a ping or a vibration from your phone. This notification is the trigger that pulls your attention away from your work. Alternatively, you might feel bored or frustrated with your task, and as a result, your mind craves a quick distraction.

- **Routine:** You check your phone. Without even thinking, you swipe open Instagram, check WhatsApp, or start watching a YouTube video. This routine is your automatic response to the trigger. You've done it so many times that it's now ingrained in your behaviour.
- **Reward:** You get a dopamine hit when you see a new message, like a funny post, or get a notification that makes you feel important. This reward feels good in the moment, which is why you return to the same behaviour the next time you're faced with the same trigger.

The Problem with the Loop

The issue with the Trigger–Routine–Reward loop is that it's designed to reinforce behaviours that are ultimately distracting and counterproductive to your goals. The problem is that your brain craves the immediate rewards (like the instant gratification of checking your phone) more than the delayed rewards that come from focused, sustained effort (like completing a task or making progress on a project).

This cycle makes it incredibly difficult to focus on long-term goals because your brain gets used to the instant gratification of distractions. It's easy to check your phone for a quick reward, but the satisfaction from completing a big task or achieving a meaningful goal doesn't always feel immediate, which makes it harder to stay focused on the task at hand.

Breaking the Loop: How to Regain Control

The key to breaking this cycle is to interrupt the loop at one of its stages—preferably the trigger stage. If you can reduce the triggers that lead to distractions, you can start to regain control over your focus and productivity.

Here's how you can break the loop:

1. Identify Your Triggers

The first step in breaking the loop is to identify your personal triggers. What are the things that prompt you to check your phone, get distracted, or procrastinate? Common triggers include:

- **Notifications:** A ping from a messaging app or a social media notification can pull your attention away from what you're doing.
- **Boredom**: When you're bored or frustrated with a task, your brain craves a quick escape in the form of distractions.
- **Stress or Anxiety**: Sometimes, you reach for your phone or find distractions as a way to avoid dealing with stress or difficult emotions.

Task: Spend a day tracking when and why you get distracted. Write down the triggers you experience, whether they're internal (like boredom) or external (like a phone notification). This will help you become more aware of when and why you break focus.

2. Disrupt the Routine

Once you've identified your triggers, it's time to disrupt the routine that follows. This involves creating new habits that will replace the old, distracting ones. Instead of automatically reaching for your phone when you're bored or stressed, you can replace that routine with something more productive or healthy.

For example:

- When you feel the urge to check your phone, instead of giving in, try going for a short walk, practicing deep breathing, or doing a quick five-minute exercise. These activities can help reframe your mind and break the automatic response.

- If you're working on a project and you're feeling bored or stuck, take a short break to refocus. Stand up, stretch, or get some fresh air before getting back to work.

Task: Choose one old routine that you know is distracting and replace it with a new, more productive activity. For instance, if you're used to checking social media when bored, try reading a book, going for a walk, or doing a quick task that helps you refocus.

3. Reward Yourself for Staying Focused

The last piece of the loop is the reward, and this is where you can change the game. The key is to provide yourself with rewards that are more aligned with your long-term goals and that help reinforce productive behaviours. Instead of giving yourself a reward that distracts you, like checking your phone, give yourself a reward that supports your focus and success.

For example:

- Reward yourself with a short break or a small treat after completing a focused work session.
- Set long-term rewards for bigger goals, like completing a project or achieving a milestone. Treat yourself to something meaningful once you've achieved it.

Task: Create a list of rewards that align with your long-term goals. These rewards should motivate you to stay on track and build better habits.

Building New, Positive Loops

The ultimate goal is to create a positive Trigger–Routine–Reward loop that helps you stay focused, productive, and aligned with your goals. By identifying your distractions, disrupting your automatic routines, and rewarding yourself for staying focused, you can create new patterns of behaviour that work in your favor.

Conclusion

The Trigger–Routine–Reward loop is a powerful cycle that shapes much of our behaviour. However, by understanding it and taking control of the triggers, routines, and rewards that drive our actions, we can break free from distractions and develop habits that support our focus and productivity. It all starts with awareness and the willingness to make small but meaningful changes to how we respond to triggers and rewards.

As you implement these strategies, you'll find that breaking the loop becomes easier with time. You'll not only regain control over your phone and distractions but also build better habits that support your long-term success and personal growth.

CHAPTER 7
Reflection Sunday

It's Sunday. For many, it's a day to relax, unwind, and take a break from the hustle of the week. But what if you used this day to reflect, recharge, and set yourself up for an even more successful week ahead? Reflection Sunday is not just about relaxation; it's about intentional growth. It's a chance to pause, look back at the past week, and evaluate how far you've come.

In this chapter, we'll explore the power of reflection and why taking time on Sundays to reflect on your progress is one of the most effective ways to stay focused, on track, and motivated. Let's dive into how you can make the most out of this crucial day.

The Power of Reflection

Reflection is one of the most powerful tools for personal growth and focus. It helps you assess your performance, recognize your achievements, identify areas for improvement, and adjust your strategies. Without reflection, it's easy to get caught up in the rush of daily life and miss the opportunity to learn from your experiences. Reflection allows you to:

- **Measure your progress:** It gives you the chance to look at where you started and how far you've come. Whether you're working on personal development, building habits, or achieving specific goals, looking back helps you appreciate your journey.
- **Identify patterns:** Reflection allows you to spot patterns in your behaviour, productivity, and distractions. You can identify what's working well and what needs to be changed. Recognizing these patterns empowers you to make better decisions moving forward.
- **Celebrate wins:** Too often, we focus on what we didn't accomplish or the challenges we faced, rather than acknowledging what we did achieve. Reflection is your opportunity to celebrate even the smallest victories, which boosts motivation and reinforces the positive habits you've built.
- **Set clearer goals:** After reflecting on your past week, you can set more realistic, actionable goals for the upcoming week. Reflection isn't just about looking back; it's about using what you've learned to move forward with clarity and purpose.

How to Make Reflection Sunday Work for You

1. Journaling: Write Down Your Thoughts

One of the most effective ways to reflect is by journaling. When you write down your thoughts, it forces you to slow down and process everything that's happened over the past week. The act of writing helps you organize your thoughts and gives you a record to look back on in the future.

Use your journal to ask yourself key questions:

- **What went well this week?** Write down the achievements, habits, or moments where you felt focused and successful. These could be big or small—whether it's completing a project, sticking to a new habit, or simply having a productive day.
- **What didn't go well?** It's just as important to identify where things didn't go according to plan. Did you get distracted often? Did you struggle with staying focused? Were there any particular moments when you lost track of your goals?
- **What were my distractions?** Reflect on the times you were distracted or unfocused. What caused these distractions? Was it a certain app, an internal feeling like boredom, or something else? Recognizing your triggers helps you address them moving forward.
- **What did I learn this week?** Every experience, good or bad, offers a lesson. What did you learn about yourself, your work habits, your focus, or your ability to manage distractions? These insights are invaluable in your journey toward self-improvement.
- **How did I feel?** Take a moment to assess your emotional state. Were you stressed, anxious, or motivated? How did your emotions affect your productivity and focus? This will help you understand how emotional well-being plays a role in your ability to stay focused.

Task: Spend 15-20 minutes journaling about the questions above. Don't rush—take your time to reflect deeply. If you need a prompt, here's one to start with: "This week, I felt most productive when..."

2. Review Your Goals

Reflection Sunday is the perfect time to check in with your goals. This isn't about overwhelming yourself with a long list of things you didn't do; rather, it's about assessing how well you're moving toward your bigger vision and adjusting your goals accordingly.

- **Review the goals you set for the week:** What did you plan to accomplish, and what did you actually achieve? Celebrate the wins, no matter how small, and be honest with yourself about where things fell short.
- **Evaluate your long-term goals:** Take a step back and consider the bigger picture. Are you on track to achieve your larger goals? Are there any changes you need to make to your approach? This is a great time to tweak your plans if needed.
- **Set new goals for the upcoming week:** Based on your reflections, set realistic and achievable goals for the coming week. Keep them specific and actionable, so that you can track your progress easily. These goals should challenge you without overwhelming you.

Task: Write down 3-5 goals for the upcoming week. Ensure that these goals are realistic, measurable, and connected to your larger purpose.

3. Self-Assessment and Accountability

Reflection Sunday isn't just about looking back—it's also about holding yourself accountable. Evaluate your commitment to your goals and routines. Did you follow through on the strategies you put in place, such as the 20-minute focus sprints or phone rules?

- **How did you manage distractions?** Review how well you stuck to your rules and routines. If you gave in to distractions, don't be hard on yourself—acknowledge it and brainstorm strategies to improve next week.
- **Were you consistent? Consistency is key to building long-term focus.** Reflect on whether you showed up every day to do the work, whether in your studies, your work, or your personal development.
- **Celebrate your progress:** If you managed to stay consistent, even with a few challenges, celebrate it! Consistency is the foundation of any successful habit, and every little bit counts.

Task: Write a self-assessment of your week. Rate yourself on a scale of 1-10 for consistency and focus. Be honest and use this as a way to motivate yourself to improve for the next week.

4. Mental Reset

Reflection Sunday is also an opportunity for a mental reset. After evaluating your progress, it's important to take some time to relax, recharge, and reset your mind for the upcoming week.

- **Disconnect:** Take a break from screens for an hour or two, or even longer if you can. Use this time to read a book, go for a walk, or meditate. A mental reset helps clear your mind and refresh your energy for the days ahead.
- **Practice gratitude:** Take a moment to reflect on the positive aspects of your week. What are you grateful for? Gratitude has been shown to improve mental health, boost motivation, and increase overall happiness.

Task: Set aside at least 30 minutes for a mental reset. Engage in an activity that helps you relax and reset, like deep breathing, stretching, or simply taking a walk outside.

The Power of Reflection for Long-Term Growth

Reflection Sunday isn't just about evaluating the past week—it's about setting yourself up for future success. When you regularly take the time to reflect on your progress, learn from your mistakes, and adjust your strategy, you are investing in your long-term growth. Reflection helps you stay aligned with your goals, build better habits, and maintain focus, all of which are critical for success.

As you continue your journey toward building focus and overcoming distractions, make Reflection Sunday a non-negotiable part of your routine. It's not just another task—it's a powerful tool that will keep you moving forward with clarity and purpose.

Conclusion

Reflection is a powerful tool for growth, and Reflection Sunday gives you a dedicated space to look back, learn, and plan for the future. By journaling your thoughts, reviewing your goals, holding yourself accountable, and resetting your mind, you will ensure that you stay on track and continue improving. Take this time seriously, and you'll find that with each Sunday, you're building a stronger, more focused version of yourself.

Task for Today: Reflect on your week. Write down your successes, challenges, and lessons. Set new goals for the upcoming week and take some time to reset mentally.

CHAPTER 8
The 20-Minute Focus Sprint

In our fast-paced world, distractions are everywhere. The constant barrage of notifications, the endless stream of information, and the pressure to multitask can make it nearly impossible to stay focused for long periods of time. However, what if I told you that you don't have to work for hours to make real progress? What if you could train your brain to stay focused for just 20 minutes at a time?

Welcome to the 20-minute focus sprint, one of the most powerful tools for boosting productivity and building lasting focus habits. In this chapter, we will explore the science behind this technique, how to implement it effectively, and why it can be a game-changer in your journey to better focus.

Why 20-Minute Focus Sprints?

The 20-minute focus sprint is grounded in the principle that the brain has limited capacity for sustained attention. The average person can only maintain peak focus for around 20 minutes before their concentration starts to wane. Trying to push yourself to work for hours at a stretch often results in burnout, frustration, and a significant decline in the quality of work. The key, then, is to work with your brain's natural rhythm, not against it.

Here's why the 20-minute sprint works:

- Brain Fatigue: When you try to focus for too long without a break, your brain starts to experience mental fatigue. This leads to a decrease in performance and an increase in distractions. The 20-minute sprint avoids this by giving your brain just enough time to engage deeply without wearing out its capacity for focus.
- **Quick Wins:** Working in short bursts allows you to experience a sense of accomplishment more frequently. Each 20-minute sprint becomes a small victory, which keeps your motivation high and reinforces the positive behaviour of sustained focus.
- **No Time to Procrastinate:** When you commit to just 20 minutes, you're less likely to procrastinate. The task seems manageable, and the small-time frame reduces the temptation to get distracted or put things off.
- **Builds Focus Over Time:** Just like physical exercise, focus can be trained and strengthened over time. The more you practice focusing for short periods, the easier it will become to stretch your attention span and work for longer periods in the future.

How to Implement the 20-Minute Focus Sprint

Now that you understand why the 20-minute sprint works, let's dive into how to effectively implement it into your daily routine.

1. Choose Your Task Wisely

Before starting your sprint, decide on a task that you want to focus on. It could be studying for an exam, working on a project, or even something as simple as reading a chapter in a book. The key is to choose something that requires your full attention, not something that you can do passively or in the background.

2. Set a Timer for 20 Minutes

This step is crucial. The timer serves as both a boundary and a commitment device. When you set a timer, you're signalling to your brain that you only have a limited amount of time to work. The time constraint triggers a sense of urgency, which can help you avoid distractions and stay on task. Use a timer app on your phone, or simply set an alarm on a traditional clock—whatever works best for you.

3. Eliminate All Distractions

Before starting your sprint, make sure that your environment is free of distractions. Turn off notifications, close any irrelevant tabs or apps, and put your phone out of reach. The goal is to create a focused, distraction-free zone for the next 20 minutes. If you can, choose a quiet space where you can concentrate fully.

4. Focus on One Task Only

During your 20-minute sprint, commit to focusing solely on the task you've chosen. Multitasking is a productivity killer, so resist the urge to check your phone, respond to messages, or switch between different tasks. If your mind starts to wander, gently redirect your attention back to the task at hand.

5. Take a 5-Minute Break

Once your 20-minute sprint is over, take a short break. Stand up, stretch, get some water, or take a few deep breaths. This is your chance to rest and reset before diving back into the next sprint. The break is essential for maintaining energy and focus throughout the day. If you plan to do multiple sprints, repeat the cycle: 20 minutes of focused work followed by a 5-minute break.

6. Track Your Progress

After each sprint, take a moment to reflect on how well you focused. Did you stay on task for the full 20 minutes, or did you get distracted? This self-awareness is key to improving your focus over time. Keep a journal or log of your daily sprints to track your progress and identify any patterns.

How to Make the Most of Your 20-Minute Sprints

While the 20-minute sprint technique is effective on its own, there are several strategies you can use to make it even more powerful.

1. Use the Pomodoro Technique

The Pomodoro Technique is a time management method that uses the 20-minute sprint approach combined with short breaks. Traditionally, the Pomodoro Technique involves working for 25 minutes and then taking a 5-minute break. However, you can adapt this to fit your needs by working in 20-minute intervals. After four sprints (or Pomodoro's), take a longer break of 15–30 minutes to recharge.

2. Pair Focus Sprints with Prioritization

To get the most out of your sprints, prioritize your most important tasks. Focus on high-priority tasks first and leave smaller, less important tasks for later. This ensures that you're using your focused energy on tasks that will have the greatest impact.

3. Use Music or White Noise

Some people find that listening to instrumental music or white noise helps them concentrate. If you're someone who thrives with background sounds, experiment with calming music or noise while doing your sprints. Just make sure the sound doesn't become a distraction itself.

4. Start Small, Then Build Up

If you're new to the 20-minute sprint method, start with just one sprint a day and gradually increase the number of sprints as you build your focus muscle. You might start with three sprints a day and work up to five or six as your capacity for focus improves.

Overcoming Challenges

Even with the best intentions, you may encounter challenges while implementing the 20-minute sprint. Here are a few common obstacles and how to overcome them:

- **Difficulty Staying Focused:** If you find it difficult to stay focused for the full 20 minutes, try breaking your task into smaller chunks. For example, instead of working on an entire project, focus on writing just one section for 20 minutes. Starting with smaller tasks can help build your concentration.
- **Getting Distracted:** If you're tempted to check your phone or get distracted during your sprint, remind yourself why you're doing it. Keep your goals in mind and remind yourself that the 20-minute sprint is a tool for

progress. If you're truly struggling, take a longer break between sprints and reset.

- **Procrastination:** If you're procrastinating, the 20-minute sprint can help break the cycle. Once you start working, it's much easier to keep going. The key is to just begin. You don't need to feel motivated to work for hours; just commit to 20 minutes, and often, the momentum will carry you further.

The Benefits of 20-Minute Focus Sprints

- Increased Productivity: By breaking your work into manageable chunks, you're more likely to get things done and avoid feeling overwhelmed.
- Better Focus: With consistent practice, you'll train your brain to focus more deeply and for longer periods of time.
- **Reduced Stress:** The sense of accomplishment after each sprint reduces the anxiety of looming tasks and deadlines.
- **Higher Motivation:** Frequent wins during your sprints will keep you motivated to continue.

Conclusion

The 20-minute focus sprint is one of the most effective ways to build and maintain focus, increase productivity, and reduce distractions. By working in short bursts and taking regular breaks, you allow your brain to work with its natural rhythms instead of against them. Over time, this approach will help you develop the mental discipline to stay focused for longer periods and accomplish more with less effort.

Task for Today: Set a timer for 20 minutes and commit to focusing on a single task without any distractions. Afterward, take a 5-minute break, then repeat. Track how many sprints you can complete in one day, and reflect on how you felt after each session.

CHAPTER 9
Habit Anchoring

In our fast-paced lives, building new habits can often feel like an uphill battle. We start strong, with good intentions, but somewhere along the way, our efforts begin to wane. Why does this happen? The truth is that forming new habits isn't just about willpower; it's about consistency and strategy. One of the most effective techniques for establishing and maintaining new habits is habit anchoring. In this chapter, we'll explore what habit anchoring is, how it works, and how you can use it to lock in lasting, productive habits that will serve you in the long run.

What Is Habit Anchoring?

Habit anchoring is a technique in which you attach a new habit to an existing one. It works by leveraging an established behaviour or routine as a "trigger" for the new habit. By anchoring a new habit to something you already do automatically, you reduce the resistance to doing the new behaviour. Over time, the new habit becomes part of your routine, just like the old one.

This approach is grounded in the principle of associative learning, which states that behaviours or events that occur together can become linked in your brain. This is the same principle that explains why you feel hungry when you see food or why your mouth waters when you smell something delicious—it's your brain associating one action with another. In habit anchoring, we use this mechanism to make the new habit feel automatic and effortless.

The Science Behind Habit Anchoring

Understanding the science behind habit formation is key to successfully using habit anchoring. The brain is wired to seek patterns, and it likes familiarity. When you pair a new behaviour with an established one, your brain begins to form a new neural connection, making the new habit easier to perform. This is because your brain's focus shifts from consciously deciding to do something to simply following the established pattern.

For example, if you want to start journaling every day, you could anchor it to something you already do without thinking, like brushing your teeth. Each time you brush your teeth, you remind yourself to journal right after. The act of brushing your teeth acts as the "trigger" or "anchor" for the new behaviour. Over time, your brain will automatically associate the two actions, and you'll begin journaling without needing to consciously decide to do it.

The Power of Habit Stacking

One popular and effective method of habit anchoring is habit stacking, a term coined by author James Clear in his book *Atomic Habits*. Habit stacking is a simple yet powerful concept that involves linking a new habit to an existing one by stacking it on top of an already established routine.

How Habit Stacking Works:

- **Identify an Existing Habit:** Start by identifying a habit you already do consistently. This could be something as simple as brushing your teeth, having a cup of coffee in the morning, or sitting down at your desk to work. These habits are often automatic and require no effort or decision-making.
- **Choose a New Habit:** Next, decide on a new habit that you want to integrate into your routine. Make sure this new habit is something specific and achievable. For example, you might want to start meditating for 5 minutes each day or write down your goals each morning.
- **Stack the New Habit on Top of the Old One**: The final step is to link the new habit to the existing one by anchoring it to the moment the old habit occurs. This means that as soon as you complete your established habit, you immediately perform the new behaviour. For example, after you brush your teeth, you could meditate for 5 minutes. Or, after you make your morning coffee, you could write down three things you're grateful for.

By stacking the new habit onto an existing one, you're creating a seamless transition from one activity to another, making it far easier to adopt and maintain the new behaviour.

How to Make Habit Anchoring Work for You

To successfully implement habit anchoring and build lasting habits, here's a step-by-step guide to get you started:

1. Choose the Right Anchor Habit

The most important part of habit anchoring is choosing the right anchor. Your anchor should be a habit that you already do consistently without thinking. This could be something as simple as brushing your teeth, drinking a glass of water, or having a cup of tea in the morning. The key is to find something that occurs at the same time every day and is deeply ingrained in your routine. The more automatic the anchor habit is, the easier it will be to pair it with a new habit.

2. Be Specific with Your New Habit

When choosing your new habit, make sure it's clear and specific. Vague goals like "I want to get more exercise" or "I want to be more productive" are too general and difficult to measure. Instead, make your new habit something concrete, like "I will do 10 push-ups after I brush my teeth" or "I will write 200 words after I sit down at my desk." The more specific you are, the easier it will be to follow through.

3. Start Small

It's important to start with small, achievable habits when you're just getting started with habit anchoring. If you try to add too much at once, you risk feeling overwhelmed and frustrated. Begin with a simple action that you can easily do every day. As the habit becomes ingrained, you can gradually increase the complexity or duration of the behaviour.

4. Set a Clear Trigger for the New Habit

Once you've identified your anchor and your new habit, it's essential to establish a clear trigger or prompt for the new behaviour. The more obvious the trigger, the better. For example, instead of "I will write in my journal," you could say, "I will write in my journal right after I brush my teeth." The specific timing and sequence will help your brain associate the two behaviours and make the new habit feel automatic.

5. Make the New Habit Enjoyable

If the new habit you're trying to form isn't enjoyable, it's going to be difficult to stick with. Try to make the habit as rewarding as possible. For example, if you're trying to meditate after your morning routine, choose a meditation app that you enjoy, or incorporate music that helps you relax. If you're journaling, use a journal with a beautiful design or fun pens to make the experience more enjoyable. The more you associate positive feelings with your new habit, the more likely you are to keep doing it.

6. Track Your Progress

Tracking your progress is an essential part of any habit-building strategy. By recording your daily progress, you hold yourself accountable and reinforce the behaviour you're trying to build. Use a habit tracker, journal, or app to log your new habit every day. Celebrate small wins along the way, as this reinforces your commitment to the new behaviour.

7. Be Consistent

Consistency is key to making habit anchoring work. The more often you repeat the behaviour, the stronger the neural connection becomes, and the easier it is to maintain the habit. Try to stick to the new habit every day, even if it's just for a short time. Over time, the habit will become automatic and part of your daily routine.

Examples of Habit Anchoring

- **Morning Routine:** After I drink my morning coffee, I will meditate for 5 minutes.
- **Exercise:** After I put on my running shoes, I will go for a 10-minute jog.
- **Reading:** After I finish my lunch, I will read one chapter of a book.
- **Productivity:** After I sit down at my desk in the morning, I will spend 10 minutes planning my day.
- **Gratitude Practice:** After I eat dinner, I will write down three things I'm grateful for.

Conclusion

Habit anchoring is a powerful technique that can help you build lasting, positive habits with minimal effort. By linking a new habit to something you already do automatically, you make it easier for your brain to accept and integrate the new behaviour into your routine. The key to success is consistency, patience, and a willingness to start small. Over time, these small habits will compound, leading to major changes in your productivity, focus, and overall well-being.

Task for Today: Identify one habit you want to add to your routine and choose an existing habit to anchor it to. Start small, be consistent, and track your progress. Reflect on how this technique helps you build the habit over time.

CHAPTER 10
Morning Setup for Focus

Your morning sets the tone for the entire day. Think of it as the foundation of your day—strong and solid, or shaky and unstable. The way you start your morning doesn't just influence your productivity for the next few hours, it also shapes your mindset, energy levels, and focus for the rest of the day. So, why not make your morning a deliberate setup for success?

In this chapter, we'll explore how you can create a morning routine that primes your brain for focus, reduces distractions, and sets you up to tackle your most important tasks with ease.

Why Morning Matters

The first few hours after you wake up are critical because they determine how you feel for the rest of the day. Your brain is still in a "transition" state, moving from a restful, dreamlike state to a more active and alert one. During this time, it's easy to fall into the trap of checking your phone, getting caught up in emails, or scrolling through social media. These distractions not only waste precious time but also hijack your focus before you've even begun your day.

By setting up your morning with intention, you signal to your brain that it's time to focus. You set the tone for your day and create habits that keep you on track. The best part? A good morning routine doesn't need to be time-consuming or complicated. It's all about making small, strategic changes that will have a big impact on your focus and productivity.

Key Elements of a Morning Setup for Focus

Creating a focused morning routine requires planning and consistency. Here are the key elements to consider:

- **Start the Day Without Your Phone**: We live in a world where our phones are a constant source of distraction. The minute we wake up, it's easy to grab our phones and get lost in notifications, messages, and social media. But this immediate exposure to external stimuli can leave us feeling anxious, distracted, and overwhelmed. It also steals away time that could be used for more productive and fulfilling activities.

Action Step: Try to avoid checking your phone for the first 30 minutes after you wake up. Instead, use this time to focus on yourself. You can start by doing something calming and intentional, like stretching, journaling, or enjoying a quiet cup of coffee. This helps you start your day with clarity, instead of diving straight into the noise of the digital world.

- **Hydrate First Thing**: After hours of sleep, your body is naturally dehydrated. Drinking water first thing in the morning not only rehydrates you but also kickstarts your metabolism and helps your brain function better. A well-hydrated brain is more alert, focused, and ready to tackle the day ahead.

Action Step: Keep a glass of water next to your bed or on your nightstand, and drink it as soon as you wake up. This simple habit can improve your energy levels and enhance your focus right from the start.

- **Incorporate Physical Movement**: Physical movement is one of the best ways to wake up your body and mind. It gets your blood flowing, increases oxygen to your brain, and helps release endorphins, which can improve mood and focus. You don't have to do a full workout—simple stretches, yoga, or even a short walk can be incredibly effective.

Action Step: Dedicate 5–10 minutes every morning to some form of movement. You could stretch your muscles, do a short yoga routine, or go for a brisk walk. Doing this will not only improve your physical health but also prepare your mind to focus and concentrate throughout the day.

- **Create a Calm, Quiet Moment**: In the rush of the day, it's easy to feel overwhelmed by the constant noise and activity around you. Giving yourself a few moments of calm and stillness in the morning can help ground you and prepare you for the day ahead. This could be a short meditation session, mindful breathing, or simply sitting in silence.

Action Step: Start your morning with 5–10 minutes of mindfulness or meditation. Focus on your breath, clear your mind, and set positive intentions for the day. If you're new to meditation, try using an app or guided session to help you get started.

- **Set Clear Intentions for the Day**: The morning is an ideal time to reflect on what you want to accomplish during the day. Setting clear intentions and goals for your day can provide you with a sense of purpose and direction. Whether it's a personal goal or a professional task, knowing what you need to focus on will help you stay on track throughout the day.

Action Step: Take a few minutes every morning to write down 3–5 key goals or tasks that you want to accomplish during the day. Make sure these goals are clear, actionable, and aligned with your long-term objectives. This will give you a sense of direction and help you stay focused.

- **Eat a Nutritious Breakfast**: Nutrition plays a crucial role in how we feel and perform throughout the day. A balanced breakfast that includes protein, healthy fats, and complex carbs can help maintain stable energy levels and improve mental clarity. Avoid sugary, processed foods that can lead to an energy crash later on.

Action Step: Aim for a balanced breakfast that includes whole grains, protein (like eggs or yogurt), and healthy fats (like avocado or nuts). This will provide sustained energy and help you maintain focus during your most important tasks.

- **Dress for Success**: The way you dress has a direct impact on your mindset. Even if you're working from home or have no meetings scheduled, dressing the part can improve your self-esteem and productivity. When you dress in a way that makes you feel confident and capable, you're more likely to take your tasks seriously and stay focused.

Action Step: Choose a morning outfit that makes you feel confident and ready to work. It doesn't have to be formal, but it should be something that signals to your brain that it's time to focus and get to work.

Example Morning Routine for Focus

Here's an example of a morning routine that primes you for focus and productivity:

- 6:00 AM – Wake up and drink a glass of water.
- 6:05 AM – Engage in 10 minutes of light stretching or yoga.
- 6:15 AM – Meditate for 5–10 minutes to calm your mind and set intentions for the day.
- 6:30 AM – Write down 3–5 key goals or tasks for the day.
- 6:40 AM – Eat a nutritious breakfast, such as oatmeal with nuts and fruit or scrambled eggs with avocado.
- 7:00 AM – Get dressed in an outfit that makes you feel confident and ready to work.
- 7:15 AM – Start working on your most important task or goal for the day.

This simple, focused morning routine ensures that you're starting your day with purpose, clarity, and energy, setting you up for a productive, focused day ahead.

Conclusion

Your morning routine is your secret weapon for achieving sustained focus and productivity throughout the day. By deliberately choosing how you spend the first few hours after waking up, you can set yourself up for success and keep distractions at bay. Remember, the key is consistency—creating a morning setup that works for you and sticking to it. In time, these habits will become second nature, allowing you to start every day with a clear, focused mind, ready to take on whatever comes your way.

Task for Today: Design your own morning setup for focus. Start by avoiding your phone for the first 30 minutes after waking up. Incorporate at least one of the other strategies, such as hydration, physical movement, or mindful reflection, into your routine. Track your progress for the next week and reflect on how it impacts your focus and productivity.

CHAPTER 11
Energy + Water + Food

The link between energy, focus, and nutrition is undeniable. Think about your body as a high-performance machine. No matter how powerful the engine, if it's not fuelled properly, it won't function at its best. The same goes for your brain and body—if you don't provide them with the right fuel, your energy, focus, and overall performance will suffer.

In this chapter, we will explore how the food you eat, the water you drink, and the energy you generate directly affect your focus, productivity, and overall well-being. By understanding the science behind these factors and making mindful choices, you can maximize your energy and maintain optimal focus throughout the day.

The Energy Equation: What You Put In, You Get Out

Every action you take during the day—from focusing on your studies to exercising or even socializing—requires energy. Your body generates energy from the food you eat, and your brain, which uses about 20% of your body's total energy, relies heavily on this fuel to operate efficiently. Without sufficient energy, both your physical and mental capabilities are compromised, leading to reduced focus, lack of motivation, and feelings of fatigue.

Therefore, understanding how to fuel your body with the right energy sources can make all the difference. Just like a car needs quality fuel to run smoothly, your body requires high-quality nutrition to function at its best.

Water: The Forgotten Essential

Water is the most underrated and yet one of the most crucial components for maintaining focus and energy. Your body is made up of approximately 60% water, and this vital resource plays a role in almost every bodily function. Water helps transport nutrients, regulate body temperature, and remove waste products from your system.

When you're dehydrated, your brain works less efficiently. Studies have shown that even mild dehydration can cause difficulty concentrating, fatigue, and irritability—three major roadblocks to maintaining focus. The longer you go without drinking water, the more your cognitive function declines, making it harder to stay sharp and energized.

Action Step: The first thing you should do when you wake up is drink a glass of water. Not only does this rehydrate your body, but it also jump-starts your metabolism and prepares you for the day. Throughout the day, aim to drink at least 8–10 cups of water. If you're engaged in physical activity, or if you're in a particularly hot environment, you may need even more.

If plain water doesn't appeal to you, try infusing it with natural flavors like lemon, cucumber, or mint to make it more interesting while still staying hydrated.

Fueling Your Brain: The Right Food Choices

What you eat plays a pivotal role in how you feel and perform throughout the day. The food you consume provides the energy your body needs, and it has a direct impact on your mental clarity, focus, and ability to sustain effort for long periods. In particular, the brain thrives on specific nutrients, such as glucose, healthy fats, vitamins, and minerals, to function at its best.

- **Complex Carbohydrates**: Carbohydrates are the body's primary energy source, and your brain uses glucose—derived from carbohydrates—as its main fuel. However, not all carbohydrates are created equal. Simple carbs, like those found in sugary snacks or white bread, provide a quick spike in energy, followed by an inevitable crash that leaves you feeling tired and sluggish. Complex carbs, on the other hand, break down more slowly, providing a steady supply of glucose that keeps you energized and focused.

Examples: Whole grains like brown rice, oats, quinoa, and whole-wheat bread are excellent sources of complex carbs. These foods provide long-lasting energy and help maintain stable blood sugar levels, avoiding the highs and lows caused by sugary foods.

- **Healthy Fats**: While fat has gotten a bad reputation in the past, not all fats are harmful. In fact, healthy fats are essential for brain health and cognitive function. The brain is made up of approximately 60% fat, and the fats you consume directly impact the efficiency of your brain cells. Omega-3 fatty acids, in particular, have been shown to support memory, focus, and mood regulation.

Examples: Fatty fishlike salmon, walnuts, chia seeds, and flaxseeds are rich in omega-3s. Avocados and olive oil are also great sources of healthy fats that can provide sustained energy.

- **Protein**: Protein is essential for muscle repair and growth, but it also plays a vital role in maintaining mental clarity and focus. Protein helps stabilize blood sugar levels and supports the production of neurotransmitters—chemicals that help brain cells communicate. Without enough protein, you may experience brain fog, lack of focus, and irritability.

Examples: Eggs, lean meats, legumes, nuts, and seeds are excellent sources of protein. Try to incorporate a serving of protein into every meal to keep your energy and focus levels high throughout the day.

- **Vitamins and Minerals**: Micronutrients like vitamins and minerals are crucial for brain health. They help convert food into energy and support brain function. In particular, B vitamins, magnesium, and iron play a significant role in maintaining mental clarity and preventing fatigue.

Examples: Leafy green vegetables, berries, nuts, seeds, and whole grains are rich in essential vitamins and minerals. These foods help support brain function and prevent nutrient deficiencies that could affect focus.

How to Structure Your Meals for Maximum Focus

Now that we understand the importance of hydration and the nutrients that fuel our brain and body, it's time to think about how to structure your meals to maximize focus and energy.

- **Breakfast:** Kick-start your day with a balanced meal that includes protein, healthy fats, and complex carbs. A nutritious breakfast can help stabilize blood sugar levels, improve concentration, and prevent mid-morning fatigue.

Example Breakfast: Oatmeal topped with chia seeds, nuts, and berries; or scrambled eggs with spinach and whole-grain toast.

- **Lunch:** Aim for a balanced lunch that will keep your energy levels high throughout the afternoon. Incorporate lean protein, whole grains, and plenty of vegetables for a nutrient-packed meal.

Example Lunch: Grilled chicken with quinoa and a side of mixed greens; or a quinoa salad with chickpeas, avocado, and olive oil.

- **Snacks:** Snacks can help keep your energy levels stable between meals. Choose nutrient-dense snacks that combine protein, healthy fats, and complex carbs.

Example Snack: A handful of almonds and a piece of fruit; or Greek yogurt with walnuts and a drizzle of honey.

- **Dinner:** Your dinner should be lighter but still provide a balance of protein, healthy fats, and vegetables. Avoid heavy or greasy foods that might leave you feeling sluggish.

Example Dinner: Baked salmon with roasted vegetables; or a stir-fry with tofu, broccoli, and brown rice.

Conclusion

Your brain and body are like any other high-performance machine: they require the right fuel to operate efficiently. By making thoughtful choices about what you eat and drink, you can improve your energy, focus, and overall performance. Water, healthy food, and proper nutrition are foundational for sustaining long-term focus and productivity.

Task for Today: Track your food and water intake for the next 24 hours. Make note of how much water you drink, what foods you consume, and how you feel throughout the day. Do you experience dips in energy or focus? Adjust your meals to ensure you're getting the right balance of hydration and nutrition.

CHAPTER 12
The Study Temple

In a world full of noise, chaos, and endless distractions, your environment becomes either your strongest ally or your biggest enemy. You can't expect to stay focused if your study space is cluttered, chaotic, or full of distractions. Just like a temple is built for peace, clarity, and devotion, your study space must be designed to promote focus, discipline, and deep work. Welcome to The Study Temple—your personal space where serious transformation begins.

This chapter will teach you how to build a powerful environment that doesn't just support your goals, but protects them. Think of this space not just as a desk or corner in your room—it's your training ground, your battlefield, and your place of mastery.

Why Your Environment Matters More Than Willpower

We often blame ourselves for a lack of focus or discipline. But what if your environment is the real reason you're distracted?

Here's the truth: your environment shapes your behaviour. If your phone is within reach, you'll check it. If snacks are in front of you, you'll eat them. If your desk is cluttered, your mind will be too.

According to behaviour science expert James Clear, "You do not rise to the level of your goals. You fall to the level of your systems." Your environment is part of that system.

The key takeaway: If you design your environment to promote focus, you won't have to *fight* distractions—they simply won't exist in your space.

Step 1: Declutter Like a Monk

Clutter is the enemy of clarity. A messy space leads to a messy mind. The first step in building your Study Temple is to remove everything that doesn't serve your focus.

Here's how to do it:

- Clear your desk of unrelated items—no random papers, books, gadgets, or decorations.
- Remove all unnecessary electronics—extra screens, video games, or even unused headphones can pull attention.
- Organize your materials—keep only the books, notebooks, and stationery you need for your current task.
- Clean your space physically—dust, wipe, and refresh. A clean space brings mental calmness.

Remember: Simplicity is power.

Step 2: Add Symbols of Purpose

Once you've decluttered, fill your Study Temple with reminders of your *why*—your reason for working hard and staying focused.

Here are some examples:

- Vision Board: Pictures, quotes, and goals that represent your dreams.
- Focus Poster: A printed sheet that says "Why I Must Focus Today" with your top 3 goals.
- Affirmation Card: A small card with powerful affirmations like "I am focused. I am disciplined. I am becoming who I was meant to be."

These elements act like mental Armor. Every time your mind wants to quit, your environment pulls you back in.

Step 3: Create Rituals in Your Space

The best athletes, musicians, and monks have one thing in common: rituals. They don't wait to "feel like it"—they train their brain to focus automatically through routine.

In your Study Temple, create a focus ritual to enter "deep work mode."

Here's a simple ritual:

- Clear desk (if not already done).
- Place water bottle on the right side.
- Open notebook and write today's focus task.

- Light a small candle or play soft instrumental music.
- Set a timer for 25 or 50 minutes and begin.

Do this every day before starting. Over time, your brain will associate this ritual with total concentration.

Step 4: Set Boundaries Around Your Temple

Your temple needs protection—physical and digital. You must set rules that keep distractions out.

Here are a few:

- No phone inside the study zone (use a drawer, another room, or app lockers).
- No social media tabs open while studying.
- Study only in this space—don't scroll or watch YouTube here. Train your brain that this space is only for growth.

If you live with family or roommates, politely explain your "focus hours" and ask not to be disturbed during those times.

Step 5: Use Tools That Enhance Focus

You don't need fancy gadgets, but a few tools can improve your study experience:

- Noise-cancelling headphones or white noise app
- Timer for Pomodoro sessions
- Sticky notes for to-dos
- Desk lamp with soft lighting

- Notebook and planner for tracking progress

Choose tools that support you, not entertain you.

Step 6: Treat It with Respect

This is where it gets real: If you treat your Study Temple like a holy place, your brain will too.

Here are some do's and don'ts:

☑ Sit with a straight back, clean clothes, and alert mind

☑ Keep water and a healthy snack nearby

☑ Clean the space after every session

☑ Say a short mantra before you begin ("I focus fully now")

✖ Don't eat full meals here

✖ Don't lie down or nap in your chair

✖ Don't multitask—one mission at a time

Make your study time sacred. Protect it like you would a prayer.

Task for Today: Build Your Study Temple

🖌 Declutter your current study space

Decorate with symbols of your purpose

- Design your focus ritual
- Remove all distractions
- Commit to studying here every day

Once you've done this, take a picture of your Study Temple and keep it as a reminder of your commitment. Whenever you feel lazy or distracted, return to this space and let it remind you: this is where your future is being built.

Final Words

A Study Temple is not just about a clean desk. It's about creating a physical symbol of your commitment to personal excellence. It's where dreams are converted into action—where you stop saying "I want to do it" and start saying "I'm doing it now."

This space is your ally. Respect it. Return to it daily. Let it become the birthplace of your next level.

This is your sanctuary. Own it.

CHAPTER 13
1-Hour Study Ritual

"Your brain performs best when it follows a ritual —not random effort."

In every great performer's life, whether it's an elite athlete, a skilled musician, or a world-class student, there exists one hidden secret: ritual. Ritual is more than just habit—it's a structured pattern that tells your mind, "It's time to focus." It reduces resistance, builds momentum, and wires your brain for peak performance.

In this chapter, we are going to install your 1-Hour Study Ritual—a structured, repeatable process that transforms your one hour of study from chaos into laser-focused productivity. This isn't about studying for long hours. It's about going deep for a short time, consistently. Because depth beats duration.

Why One Hour?

Your brain doesn't need 6 hours of study at once. In fact, trying to focus for that long usually leads to distraction, burnout, or wasted time. But one hour of deep, focused study—done properly—can often produce more than 3–4 hours of distracted effort.

One hour is long enough to go deep, and short enough to maintain intensity. It's the perfect focus unit.

The goal is simple: Build one daily, high-quality, 60-minute session that becomes your non-negotiable routine.

The Study Ritual Blueprint (5 Phases)

Your 1-Hour Study Ritual has five parts:

- Pre-Study Ritual (5 minutes)
- First Focus Block (25 minutes)
- Short Break (5 minutes)
- Second Focus Block (25 minutes)
- Wrap-Up Ritual (5 minutes)

Let's go through each.

---

1. Pre-Study Ritual (5 Minutes)

Before you start studying, your brain needs a clear signal: "*We are about to enter focus mode.*"

Here's what to do:

- Clean your desk — remove clutter and unnecessary items
- Put your phone on silent or outside the room

- Take a few deep breaths or do 1 minute of mindful breathing
- Write down your study goal for this session — What will you complete in the next hour?

This short pre-study phase prepares your body and brain for full engagement. It eliminates decision fatigue and builds a habit of intentional effort.

---

2. First Focus Block (25 Minutes)

This is where deep work begins.

Set a timer for 25 minutes and start your task. The rule here is no interruptions, no multitasking. Only one goal—total focus.

Tips for maximum focus:

- Use a physical book or notes instead of digital when possible
- Close all browser tabs not related to your task
- Keep water nearby to avoid getting up
- If a distracting thought arises, write it down on a distraction sheet instead of acting on it

This 25-minute sprint trains your brain to focus fully. Over time, your mental stamina increases like a muscle.

---

3. Short Break (5 Minutes)

Once the first block ends, take a 5-minute break.

But be careful—don't open social media or lie in bed. That will break your rhythm. Use this time for:

- Stretching or walking around
- Drinking water or having a light snack
- Closing your eyes for a moment
- Breathing exercises or fresh air

This break helps reset your brain without overstimulation.

---

4. Second Focus Block (25 Minutes)

Now go back in. Another 25-minute sprint, just like before.

You'll notice something powerful here: the second sprint often feels easier than the first. Your brain is warmed up. You're in the zone. You'll produce more, understand better, and feel less distracted.

Stick to the same rules: no interruptions, full focus, and one task at a time.

---

5. Wrap-Up Ritual (5 Minutes)

The hour ends with closure.

Here's your 5-minute wind-down ritual:

- Review what you completed
- Write one line about what you learned
- Write one question that came up during study

- Rate your focus on a scale of 1–10
- Plan your next session topic

These small ritual builds reflection and continuity, and it reinforces progress in your mind.

Your Task: Complete One 1-Hour Study Ritual Today

- ☑ Clean your space
- ☑ Follow the 5-phase ritual exactly
- ☑ Use a timer (phone, clock, or app)
- ☑ Track your focus rating at the end

Even if you've never done a focused study session before, this ritual will change your perspective. It builds flow, confidence, and momentum. It helps your brain associate study time with full engagement—not stress, multitasking, or frustration.

What to Expect After a Week of Ritual

If you do this for 7 days straight, here's what you'll start to notice:

- Your mental fatigue will decrease
- You'll start to look forward to study time
- Your focus span will grow naturally
- You'll build more output in less time

- You'll trust yourself more—because you're showing up

The 1-Hour Study Ritual is the foundation of mastery. Whether you're preparing for exams, learning a new skill, or trying to build a career—this simple daily hour can shape your entire future.

Final Words

This is not about forcing yourself to study for hours. It's about *training* your mind to love deep work. Your focus is your superpower. But like any superpower, it requires training, structure, and intention.

The ritual is your weapon. Respect it. Protect it. And repeat it.

Do your 1-Hour Study Ritual today—and begin the process of rewiring your brain for greatness.

This is how legends study.

CHAPTER 14
Week 2 Review

"You're not lazy. You just needed clarity."

The end of Week 2 is more than just a checkpoint—it's a powerful mirror. Two weeks ago, you started this journey to master your focus. You didn't just read words. You took action. You studied with a timer. You installed rituals. You decluttered your environment. You experimented with new habits.

This chapter is not about adding anything new. It's about looking back with honesty, celebrating progress, and most importantly, identifying what actually worked for *you*.

Because the truth is this: Not all strategies work for everyone. The only way to know what's truly effective for your brain, your lifestyle, and your goals is through reflection and self-review.

Let's dive into your Week 2 Focus Review.

Part 1: What Did You Learn About Your Focus?

Ask yourself the following questions and write down your answers in a notebook or journal:

- When during the day did you feel the most focused?
- What specific habit improved your focus the most this week?
- Which task or day felt hardest to complete, and why?
- What part of the 1-Hour Study Ritual worked best for you?
- Were there any distractions that kept showing up, even after rules were set?

These questions aren't just for analysis—they help you develop self-awareness, which is one of the top traits of high performers. The more you understand your patterns, the more you can control them.

Part 2: Your Weekly Focus Score

On a scale of 1–10, rate yourself for each of these:

Area	Your Score (1–10)
Consistency in showing up to study	
Energy levels during study sessions	
Phone usage control	
Morning focus routine	
Evening distraction control	
Study ritual implementation	

Area	Your Score (1–10)
Journal/Reflection habits	
Nutrition + water + rest	
Ability to delay urges	
Overall sense of focus	

Now, calculate your average score. That number doesn't define you. It guides you. If you're scoring below 6, that's a signal to review your friction points. If you're above 7, build on that momentum.

Part 3: What Helped You the Most?

Pick 3 things that you believe made the biggest difference in your week.

Examples could include:

- The 20-Minute Focus Sprint
- Morning no-phone rule
- Decluttering the study area
- Eating healthier snacks
- Anchoring journaling with brushing

Once you identify these, commit to locking them in. These are now part of your personal Focus Formula.

Part 4: What Needs Improvement?

Every growth phase reveals a few weak spots.

What didn't work this week?

- Were you inconsistent with your phone rules?
- Did you skip your morning setup a few times?
- Was your energy crashing after lunch?

Be honest, not harsh. Awareness > Judgment.

Now write one line for each area that needs improvement and one action step to fix it in Week 3.

Example:

❌ Weak Area: I kept using the phone in bed again.

✅ Fix: Put phone across the room before sleeping.

Part 5: Your Focus Reflection Journal

Now write a short paragraph answering these two prompts:

- "What is changing in me?"
- "What do I want to master by the end of next week?"

Let this be your personal letter to yourself. It can be messy, real, vulnerable. The power is not in perfection—it's in reflection.

Part 6: Share Your Journey (Optional but Powerful)

If you're doing this challenge with a group, share your review highlights:

- Your top 3 helpful habits
- Your average Focus Score

- Your biggest internal change

This step builds accountability and creates a shared momentum. When you speak your wins and struggles out loud (or in writing), they become real—and more powerful.

Final Words: You're Not Lazy—You're Learning

Let's say this out loud:

"I am not lazy. I am learning how to structure my mind, my environment, and my habits. Focus is a skill—and I'm building it."

You've now completed two weeks of deep work, self-awareness, and habit installation. That's not ordinary. That's rare. You're separating yourself from the crowd, one ritual, one decision, and one hour at a time.

Week 3 is where we go deeper—not harder. We'll learn how to master thoughts, emotions, and temptations. But for now, take this moment to breathe and feel proud of the progress you've made.

Your journey is real. Your brain is changing. Your future is being built—one focused day at a time.

You're doing great. Keep going.

CHAPTER 15

Thought Control 101

"You are not your thoughts. You are their master."

Distraction is not just about phones, apps, or loud environments. The greatest battle is happening inside your mind—between the thoughts you want and the thoughts that show up uninvited.

Today's chapter is about taking back control over that inner battlefield.

Let's be clear: You cannot control which thoughts appear in your mind. But you can absolutely control how you respond to them.

This is the real superpower of focused individuals—they don't chase every thought. They observe. They pause. They decide.

Let's understand how to master this.

Why Thoughts Distract You

Every time you try to focus, your brain does something curious. It starts throwing random thoughts at you:

- "I should check my messages."
- "What if I miss something important?"
- "I'm bored. Let me scroll for 2 minutes."

Sound familiar?

These aren't just accidents. They are patterns built over years of impulsive phone use, multitasking, and emotional avoidance.

Here's what's happening:

- Trigger – You sit down to study.
- Mental Habit – Brain searches for a dopamine hit.
- Thought Appears – "Open that app. It'll take 30 seconds."
- You Obey – Focus is broken. Again.

But what if, at step 3, you paused?

The Power of Observation

Most people react automatically to thoughts. But focused individuals do something else: they observe their thoughts like clouds passing in the sky.

Thought appears → You notice it → You *don't* obey.

This small pause changes everything.

Try saying:

- "That's just a thought. I don't have to believe it."
- "Interesting—my brain wants distraction. But I don't."

You don't fight thoughts. You see them, label them, and let them go.

This is called meta-awareness—being aware that you're thinking, while you're thinking. It's what monks train for years. But you can start practicing it today.

---

3 Types of Distracting Thoughts

Let's break down the common types of thoughts that ruin your focus:

- **Urgency Thoughts**
  "Check that notification right now!"

  ➤ These thoughts trick your brain into believing something terrible will happen if you don't check instantly.

- **Escape Thoughts**
  "This is boring. Let's do something fun."

  ➤ Your brain resists hard tasks and looks for comfort. This is where most students give up.

- **Self-Doubt Thoughts**
  "I'm not good at this. What's the point?"

  ➤ These are the most dangerous—they attack your confidence and make distraction feel justified.

Your task is not to eliminate them (you can't). Your task is to identify and interrupt them.

The 4-Step Thought Control Method

Whenever a distracting thought hits you during focus time, use this 4-step formula:

1. Notice It.

Say silently: "I just had a thought."

2. Name It.

Label it: "That's an escape thought." or "That's self-doubt."

3. Neutralize It.

Say: "Thanks, brain. I'm choosing not to follow that."

4. Redirect.

Gently bring your attention back to your current task.

This simple method builds mental muscles. With practice, you'll find you can resist most distractions before they take over.

Thought Journal Exercise (Today's Task)

For the next 24 hours, do this:

- Keep a small notebook or your journal nearby.
- Every time a distracting thought comes, pause and write:
    - The time
    - The exact thought
    - What type it was (Urgency, Escape, Self-Doubt)
    - Whether you followed it or resisted

Example Entry:

- 2:45 PM – "Check WhatsApp, maybe there's an update" – Urgency – Resisted

After 24 hours, review your journal. You'll be amazed by how many times your brain tries to pull you away—and how often you can say "No."

Building Mental Discipline

Mental control is like physical training. You don't build it by reading about it. You build it by showing up every day and doing the rep.

Each time you resist a thought; your brain rewires itself.

Neuroscience calls it neuroplasticity—the ability of your brain to change and adapt. And this power is already working for you, right now.

A Note on Compassion

You will still get distracted. You will still follow a few thoughts. That's okay. The goal is not perfection. The goal is awareness and growth.

Don't shame yourself. Just return to focus gently.

"I noticed. I wandered. I'm back."

This mantra can carry you through the hardest focus sessions.

Final Reflection

Write in your journal:

- What thought distracted you the most today?
- Which thought type do you struggle with most (Urgency, Escape, Self-Doubt)?
- What phrase can you use to remind yourself that *you are not your thoughts*?

Some examples:

- "My brain offers thoughts. I decide which ones to follow."
- "This discomfort will pass. I don't need a distraction."
- "Silence is not emptiness. It's focus in progress."

You now have one of the most powerful tools of mental strength: thought control.

You're not weak for getting distracted. You're strong for noticing and choosing differently.

Let the thoughts come. But don't let them rule you.

You are the thinker—not the thought.

CHAPTER 16
Delay = Power

"Every time you delay a temptation by 10 minutes, you weaken it."

There's a golden rule that almost every focused, high-performing person lives by—they don't react instantly. They pause, even for a few seconds. That pause is where all the power lives.

In this chapter, you'll learn the science and strategy behind delaying impulses and how that simple habit can give you back control over your phone, your distractions, and your life.

The Impulse That Destroys Focus

Imagine this:

You're studying. You feel slightly bored. Suddenly a thought hit—

"Let me check Instagram. Just for 2 minutes."

Your hand reaches for the phone... and 30 minutes are gone.

This is how it happens—every single day.

You don't *decide* to waste 30 minutes. You just *don't pause*. You obey the first impulse.

Distraction is not a decision. It's a reflex. And the way to break that reflex? Delay it.

The Power of a 10-Minute Delay

Here's the rule:

Whenever you feel the urge to check your phone, scroll, snack, or escape—just delay it for 10 minutes.

Don't say no forever. Just say "not now."

This 10-minute window does 3 things:

- **Interrupts the automatic loop:** It breaks the chain between thought and action.
- **Gives your rational brain a chance:** The logical part of your brain (prefrontal cortex) gets time to catch up and say, "Wait… why?"
- **Weakens the craving**: Most urges peak and then drop if not fed immediately.

Researchers call this the "urge surfing" method. Like a wave, urges rise, crash, and fade. Your job is not to fight them—just ride them out.

Real-Life Examples of the Delay Rule

Let's see how this looks in action:

- Urge: "I want to watch YouTube Shorts.": Response: Set a timer for 10 minutes. Focus on your current task. After 10 minutes, ask: *Do I still want this?*

- Urge: "I want to message a friend during study.": Response: Write it down. Tell yourself: "I'll do this after the session."
- Urge: "Let me check notifications.": Response: Put phone face down. Breathe. Wait 10 minutes.

In 80% of the cases, the urge disappears.

And even if it doesn't—you've already built discipline by not giving in instantly. That's massive progress.

Why Delaying Builds Willpower

Your willpower is like a battery. Every time you resist an urge, you strengthen it.

Think of your brain in two parts:

- The fast brain (impulsive, emotional, reactive)
- The slow brain (rational, focused, self-controlled)

When you delay, you shift control from the fast brain to the slow brain.

This shift isn't magic—it's biology. And it's trainable.

The 3 Levels of the Delay Skill

Like any skill, delaying temptation has levels. Where are you now?

Level 1 – Reaction
You feel the urge and instantly act. No pause.

Level 2 – Awareness
You feel the urge and *notice* it. Sometimes you still act, sometimes not.

Level 3 – Control

You feel the urge, notice it, and consciously delay it—even if only for 1 minute.

Your goal isn't to kill the urge. It's to become stronger than it.

Today's Practice: The 10-Minute Delay Challenge

For the next 12 hours, follow this:

- Every time you feel an urge to do something distracting (scroll, snack, open a tab):
    - Pause.
    - Set a timer for 10 minutes.
    - Stay on your task or do something else productive during the wait.
    - After the timer, ask: *Do I still want this?*
- Track it in your journal. Note:
    - Time
    - What the urge was
    - Whether you gave in or delayed
    - What happened after 10 minutes

Example Entry: 4:15 PM – Urge to open YouTube – Delayed – Urge disappeared, stayed focused on reading.

At the end of the day, reflect: How many urges faded? How much time did you save?

Delayed Gratification = Lifelong Power

This is bigger than study or screens.

The most successful people in life—athletes, CEOs, creators—all have one thing in common:

They can delay pleasure now to earn a bigger reward later.

This is called delayed gratification, and it's been proven to predict success better than IQ or talent.

The famous Stanford "marshmallow experiment" showed that kids who could wait 15 minutes for a second marshmallow grew up to have:

- Better grades
- Higher incomes
- Stronger relationships
- Greater mental health

All because they could wait.

Create a "Delay Toolkit"

Here's what to do *during* your 10-minute wait:

- Drink water
- Take 10 deep breaths
- Read one page of a book
- Walk around your room
- Write a quick journal entry
- Do 10 push-Ups

The idea is to keep your body and mind occupied while the urge cools down.

Final Words

Discipline doesn't mean you never feel temptation.

It means you've trained yourself to pause before acting.

That pause is where the average life ends—and the extraordinary life begins.

So next time the urge hits… don't say "no."

Just say, "*Later.*"

That's enough to win.

CHAPTER 17
The 'Why' Wall

"When you remember your purpose, distractions die."

You don't have a focus problem.

You have a clarity problem.

Every time you lose focus, it's because your "why" is not loud enough.

In this chapter, you'll discover the power of purpose, and how to build a physical reminder of your mission—a "Why Wall"—that pulls you out of distractions and pushes you into your best self every single day.

Why You Get Distracted So Easily

Let's be honest.

You already know what's good for you. You know studying is important. You know phones are a distraction.

You know wasting time won't help your dreams.

So why do you still do it?

Because your brain is wired to chase what feels urgent—not what's important.

And in moments of boredom, stress, or laziness, your mind forgets why you started.

That's where your Why Wall comes in.

What is a "Why Wall"?

A Why Wall is not just decoration. It's your *fuel station*.

It's a wall, board, or section of your room where you put visual reminders of why you want to focus, study, grow, and win.

This is where your reasons live.

When your motivation drops or distractions rise, this wall becomes your shield.

What to Include on Your Why Wall

Here's what belongs on a real, personal Why Wall:

1. Your Top 3 Reasons to Stay Focused

Example:

- "I want to give my parents a better life."
- "I refuse to live an average life."
- "I want to become a doctor who saves lives."

Write them big. Write them bold.

2. Photos that Trigger Emotion

- A picture of your family
- Your dream college or career
- A childhood photo to remind you how far you've come

3. Quotes that Punch Your Soul

Find words that hit hard. Examples:

- "If you get tired, learn to rest—not quit."
- "One day, this pain will become your power."
- "Success is rented. Rent is due every day."

4. Your Dream Life Description

Write a short paragraph:

"In 5 years, I will be living in my dream city, earning well, supporting my parents, and feeling proud of who I became."

Read this aloud every week.

How to Build It

Step 1: Choose Your Space.

Pick a wall near your study area. A clear corner. A section above your desk.

Step 2: Design It.

Use sticky notes, printouts, sketches, string lights, or a pin board. Make it *your vibe*.

Step 3: Add Layer by Layer.

Start with one quote today. Then a reason tomorrow. Build it over a few days. No pressure.

Step 4: Make It Visible.

You should be able to *see* your Why Wall the moment you enter the room. Visibility = power.

The Science Behind It

Your brain is visual. It responds better to images than to thoughts.

- A goal written and seen daily is 42% more likely to be achieved.
- Emotional visuals activate your limbic system—the part that drives motivation and action.
- Repetition creates mental anchors. The more you see your "why," the more your brain believes it.

In short: your Why Wall turns your goals from a *vague idea* into a *daily reality*.

When to Use the Why Wall

- When you feel lazy or bored
- When you want to quit
- Before starting a study session
- After failing a test or missing a target
- Whenever you ask, "What's the point?"

Don't just look at it—read it aloud. Remind yourself what's at stake.

Today's Task: Build Your Why Wall

- Take 30 minutes today to start your wall.
- Write 3 big reasons you MUST stay focused.
- Find or print at least one powerful image or quote.
- Stick it where you'll see it every day.
- Share a picture with your focus group/accountability partner if you have one.

Optional: Record a 1-minute voice note stating your "Why" and play it on tough days.

Real Story: Aarav's Wall

Aarav, 16, used to waste 5–6 hours daily on gaming and YouTube. He felt stuck.

One day, after a tough conversation with his mom, he wrote this on his wall:

"I will never let my parents cry because of me again."

He stuck a picture of his family next to it. Every time he looked at it, something shifted.

He didn't become perfect overnight, but he started *winning the daily battles*.

Your wall can do the same.

Final Reminder

Discipline will fail. Motivation will disappear.

But your "Why" will stay—if you can see it, feel it, and revisit it every day.

So build your Why Wall not just as a decoration—but as your battle armour.

Every time you forget what you're fighting for... look up. Your future is staring right back at you.

CHAPTER 18
Boring is Powerful

"Don't fear boredom—it is where your future lives."

If you really want to change your life, here's a truth you must swallow:

Success is hidden in boring moments.

The world teaches you to chase excitement, stimulation, and novelty every minute. But growth, mastery, and greatness? They're slow. Repetitive. Quiet. And yes—boring.

This chapter is your invitation to rewire your relationship with boredom. It's not your enemy. It's your greatest opportunity.

Why You Hate Boredom

Let's break it down.

Your brain is addicted to *dopamine spikes*—those little hits of excitement you get when something new happens. A funny reel. A surprise message. A game level-up.

The modern world has trained you to expect constant entertainment. The result?

- You can't sit still.
- You can't be alone with your thoughts.
- You can't study unless something is "interesting."
- You feel *restless* if you're not stimulated.

But here's the thing: real work is boring.

And that's not a flaw. That's a feature.

Boring is Where Magic Happens

Ask any athlete, artist, doctor, or entrepreneur—what made you world-class?

Their answer won't be:

"It was so exciting every day!"

It'll be:

"I repeated the same thing until I couldn't get it wrong."

The repetition—the quiet, focused, disciplined work—is boring.

But it's also where:

- Muscles are built
- Concepts are mastered
- Habits are formed
- Confidence is developed

If you run away from boredom, you run away from all of this.

The Hidden Superpower of Silence

Let's take it deeper.

Most people are afraid of silence.

Why?

Because silence brings them face to face with themselves. Their thoughts. Their guilt. Their fears.

So they stay busy. Always scrolling, watching, chatting, moving.

But in silence:

- You get clarity.
- You process pain.
- You unlock creativity.
- You begin healing.

The most successful people in the world schedule silence. They don't avoid boredom—they seek it out.

What Happens When You Don't Fear Boredom

Once you stop fearing boredom and start embracing it, a shift happens.

- You stop chasing dopamine, and start building discipline.
- You stop needing motivation, and start relying on consistency.

- You stop complaining about focus, and start creating depth.

You start winning—slowly, silently, but surely.

Task of the Day: The 10-Minute Silence Challenge

Today, your only task is this:

Sit in silence for 10 minutes.

No phone. No music. No talking.

Just you, your breath, your thoughts.

This will feel awkward. Painful, even.

But stay.

Watch the thoughts come and go.

Feel the itch to "do something"—and resist it.

By doing nothing, you're doing something extraordinary: You're training your mind to be present, calm, and in control.

You are teaching your brain that it does not always need stimulation to feel alive.

Bonus: How to Train Your Boredom Muscle Daily

Make peace with boredom by practicing it in small doses:

- Walk without your phone.
- Eat without watching anything.
- Wait in a queue without scrolling.
- Study even when it feels dry.

Every time you endure boredom; your *concentration muscle* grows stronger.

Journal Prompt

After your 10-minute silence session, write down:

- What did I feel?
- What thoughts came up?
- Did I feel anxious, bored, calm, or something else?
- How can I sit in silence more regularly?

There is no wrong answer. This is about building awareness.

Real Story: Meera's Breakthrough

Meera, 17, used to switch between apps every few seconds while studying.

She couldn't sit for more than 5 minutes.

After reading about silence, she started doing 10 minutes of stillness daily.

The first week? Torture.

But then, something changed. Her anxiety dropped. Her thoughts became clearer. She stopped craving constant noise.

Now, she calls her daily silence:

"My recharge time."

You can experience this too.

Final Words

Most people will continue to fear boredom—and so they'll remain slaves to distraction.

But not you.

If you can learn to sit through silence, boredom, and repetition, you unlock something rare:

The ability to focus even when it's not exciting.

And that is where your future is hiding.

CHAPTER 19

Declutter Your Mind

"Too many tabs open in your brain?"

Have you ever felt like your brain has 27 tabs open—and 26 of them are frozen?

You sit down to study, but instead of focusing, your mind jumps to:

- "I need to reply to that message."
- "Did I charge my phone?"
- "What if I fail this exam?"
- "Why hasn't that person texted me back?"

It's like your thoughts are running wild in the background. Noisy. Unorganized. Endless.

This chapter is your turning point.

It's time to declutter your mind—just like you would declutter a messy room.

The Mental Mess

Most people walk around with a cluttered mental desktop:

- Incomplete tasks
- Unspoken feelings
- Unfinished conversations
- Future worries
- Random thoughts

This constant mental chatter is not just annoying—it's *exhausting*. It drains your brain's processing power. It kills your focus. And it increases your anxiety.

You can't focus on what matters when everything feels urgent.

So today, we do something radical: We empty the mental junk drawer.

The Power of the Brain Dump

There's a simple yet powerful tool for mental clarity. It's called a brain dump.

Here's how it works:

You grab a pen and paper (or a blank note app).
You set a timer for 10 minutes.
And then—you write.
No filter. No structure. No grammar. Just *everything* that's in your head.

Write down:

- Things you need to do

- Things you're worried about
- People you're thinking about
- Ideas floating in your mind
- Conversations you're rehearsing
- Anything that feels "open" or incomplete

The goal is not to solve anything.

The goal is to get it out of your head and onto a page.

Why This Works

Your brain is not built to hold everything.

It's built to process things one at a time.

But when you leave 50 things "open" in your mind, your brain gets overwhelmed. It constantly tries to remind you of incomplete tasks or emotional loops—like background apps draining your battery.

The brain dump:

- Frees up mental RAM
- Reduces stress
- Increases focus
- Improves emotional clarity

It's like cleaning your desk before you begin deep work.

Task of the Day: 10-Minute Brain Dump

Today, do this:

- Set a 10-minute timer.

- Write nonstop—don't worry about structure.
- Include everything: tasks, thoughts, feelings, doubts, excitement—anything!

Optional:

- Use bullet points.
- Use categories like "To Do," "Worries," "Random," or "Reminders."
- Once you're done, highlight 1–2 items that are actually important. Let the rest go.

You'll feel a surprising amount of peace just from doing this once.

What to Do After the Dump

Once you've cleared your mind:

- Don't rush back into chaos.
- Sit with the quiet for a minute.
- Then choose *one thing* to focus on.

That's the real secret:

When your mind isn't juggling everything, it can give its full power to *anything*.

Real Story: Raghav's Mind Reset

Raghav, 19, was stuck in the spiral of procrastination. His grades were slipping, and he thought he had an attention problem.

But the truth? His brain was overloaded with:

- Part-time job worries

- Family pressure
- Fear of failure
- 12 unfinished tasks

When he did his first brain dump, he cried. Not because it was hard—but because he realized how much he was *carrying silently*.

He started doing a brain dump every Sunday. Now he says:

"It's like sweeping my brain clean before the week starts."

You can experience this too.

Journal Prompt

After your brain dump, answer:

- What surprised me about what I wrote?
- What is actually *urgent* or *important*?
- What can I let go of?

Remember: Just because it popped up in your mind doesn't mean it deserves your energy.

Make It a Weekly Ritual

Start making brain dumps a Sunday habit. It helps you:

- Reset for the week
- Organize your thoughts
- Spot emotional clutter
- Focus on what matters

You'll feel lighter. Calmer. Clearer.

Final Thoughts

Your brain is not Google Chrome.
It's not meant to run 30 tabs at once.

Declutter your mind and give it the space to think deeply.

Because a clear mind is a focused mind.
And a focused mind is an unstoppable force.

CHAPTER *20*
Digital Minimalism

"What if your phone had only useful apps?"

Your smartphone is one of the most powerful tools in your life.

It's also one of the biggest enemies of your focus.

Let's be honest—most of us don't *use* our phones; our phones use *us*.

We unlock them without reason. We scroll without thinking. We jump from app to app, notification to notification, like puppets controlled by algorithms.

Digital Minimalism isn't about quitting technology. It's about taking control.

It's about using digital tools intentionally, not habitually.

In this chapter, we'll learn how to turn your phone from a source of distraction into a tool of focus and growth.

What Is Digital Minimalism?

Digital Minimalism is a lifestyle where you only keep digital tools and apps that support your values and goals, and eliminate everything else.

The concept was popularized by Cal Newport, who defined it as:

"A philosophy of technology use in which you focus your online time on a small number of carefully selected and optimized activities."

This is not about being anti-tech.

It's about being pro-purpose.

If an app helps you study better, learn a new skill, stay connected meaningfully—that's great.

But if it's draining your time, attention, and peace—it's got to go.

Why Your Digital Life Needs a Cleanup

Here's what happens when you carry 100 apps:

- Constant buzzing = constant anxiety.
- Every idle moment = scrolling time.
- Focus gets chopped into 10-second slices.
- Your brain never rests. It never goes deep.

The truth is: You don't need more apps. You need more clarity.

Today's Challenge: The 10 App Rule

Here's what you're going to do today:

Only keep 10 essential apps on your home screen.

These apps should:

- Help you grow.
- Save your time.
- Bring genuine joy or connection.

All other apps?

Move them to the app drawer. Or delete them.

Your home screen should feel clean, intentional, and peaceful—not like a battlefield of icons screaming for your attention.

How to Decide What Stays

Use these questions for each app:

- Does this app align with my goals?
- Does it serve me—or does it steal from me?
- When I use it, do I feel better or worse afterward?

Keep:

- Calendar
- Notes
- Study apps (like Notion, Google Docs, PDF readers)
- Essential communication (calls, maybe one messaging app)

- Music or meditation (if it helps you focus)

Move or delete:

- Social media apps
- Shopping apps
- News or meme apps
- Anything that thrives on your impulsiveness

Remember: Just because something is popular doesn't mean it's good for you.

Real Life: Minimalist Phone, Focused Mind

Tanya, a 17-year-old student preparing for NEET, shared her experience:

"I deleted all social media, kept only WhatsApp, Calendar, and a PDF reader. At first, I felt empty. But within a week, my mind was calmer. I had hours I didn't know existed."

That's the hidden power of digital minimalism—you don't just remove apps; you reclaim time and mental energy.

Beyond the Phone: Apply It Everywhere

This principle isn't just for your phone. You can apply it to:

- Your laptop (too many tabs? too many files?)
- Your notifications (turn off all but the essential)
- Your digital habits (scrolling before sleep, random YouTube spirals)

Ask yourself:

"Is this digital behaviour helping me become who I want to be?"

Journal Prompt

After decluttering your phone, answer these:

- Which 3 apps steal most of my time and energy?
- How did I feel when I cleaned up my screen?
- What can I do with the time I've freed up?

A Clean Digital Space = A Clearer Life

When your phone is clean and quiet:

- You stop reacting to every buzz.
- You start thinking more deeply.
- You return to your real life, your real goals.

Digital minimalism is not a one-time act—it's a mindset.

From today, don't just own your phone. Rule it.

Because when you remove the digital junk, you make room for real growth, peace, and purpose.

Task of the Day:

☑ Keep only 10 essential apps on your home screen.

☑ Remove, hide, or uninstall the rest.

☑ Sit in silence for 5 minutes and feel the difference.

CHAPTER 21
Sunday Reflection

"You're now 70% done. Let's check who you've become."

It's Sunday again.

But this Sunday is different from the first one you experienced in Chapter 7.

Back then, you had just begun the journey. You were wrestling with your habits, facing distractions every few minutes, and probably feeling unsure about whether you could even complete these 30 days.

Today, you're standing at the 70% milestone.

Two weeks from now, you'll be done with the program.

But before we move forward, let's pause.

Let's look backward, inward—and measure not just progress, but transformation.

Because consistency means nothing if it doesn't change you.

Why Reflection Is a Superpower

In our hyper-fast, always-on lives, we rarely stop to ask:

- What changed in me this week?
- What is no longer part of my life?
- What has become stronger inside me?

Reflection turns experience into insight.

It turns actions into identity.

Without reflection, we just go through routines.

With reflection, we grow through every moment.

The Focus Journey So Far

Let's review what you've already accomplished:

- [x] You've identified your distractions.
- [x] You've reset your dopamine system.
- [x] You've cleaned your digital life.
- [x] You've installed powerful focus habits.
- [x] You've started rewiring your brain.

You're not the same person who began this challenge. You've likely become:

- Less reactive
- More intentional
- More aware

- More confident in your ability to *focus on what matters*

Journal Reflection: Deep Questions

Take your notebook. Take 30 minutes. Be honest, raw, and unfiltered.

Answer these:

- What's the biggest internal change I've felt in the past 3 weeks?
- What habit was hardest to break? And how did I manage it?
- Which chapter/task felt like a turning point for me? Why?
- How do I feel when I'm focused versus when I'm distracted?
- What is one distraction that still has power over me? What will I do about it this week?

Share Your Transformation (If You're in a Group)

If you're doing this journey with a community, friend, or mentor—share your insights.

Reflection becomes even more powerful when it's expressed.

It helps others see what's possible.
It holds you accountable.
And it reminds you: *you are not alone in this journey.*

You Are Becoming the Focused Version of You

This isn't about becoming perfect.

It's about becoming clear.

You're learning that:

- Focus is not natural—it's trained.
- Distractions don't disappear—you manage them.
- Success is not about hacks—it's about habits.

And most importantly:

You've proven to yourself that you're capable of change.

Your Task Today

- Sit with yourself for 30 minutes in silence. No phone. No music. No journal.
- After that, write your answers to the reflection questions above.
- If you're comfortable, share them with someone you trust—or write a letter to your future self.

What's Ahead?

The final week is coming.

In this last phase, we'll build a lifestyle of focus—a system you can carry for months and years, not just 30 days.

No more temporary fixes.

We'll build a Focus-for-Life Blueprint.

But before that, appreciate what you've already done. Take pride. Take a breath. Take ownership of your journey.

Quote to Remember:

"You don't change in a day. You change daily. And one day, you wake up transformed."

CHAPTER 22

The 5AM Rule (Even at 7AM)

"It's not about waking up early—
it's about owning your morning."

There's a rule that says: "The early bird gets the worm."

But in the world of productivity, that statement has been taken to a whole new level. Countless high achievers, from successful entrepreneurs to Olympians, swear by their early morning routines. But here's the catch—you don't need to wake up at 5 AM to win your day.

The goal isn't just waking up early; it's about owning your morning and setting the tone for the rest of your day. It's about giving yourself a head start before the distractions of the world rush in. The 5 AM rule can be adapted to fit your schedule, even if you're not a morning person. So, whether your 5 AM is at 6:30 or 7 AM, it's time to make your mornings intentional and focused.

Why Mornings Matter

Your morning routine is the foundation of your day. The first few hours set the mood and energy level for everything that follows. If you wake up feeling rushed or stressed, your whole day follows suit.

On the flip side, if you start your day with intention, you will likely experience:

- Improved focus throughout the day
- A sense of control and accomplishment
- Greater mental clarity and energy
- An early win that boosts self-confidence and motivation

Mornings are the most important part of your day because they shape your mindset. The way you begin your morning can dictate your entire approach to challenges, tasks, and productivity.

The Power of a Morning Routine

A morning routine serves as a blueprint for success. It gives you the power to set the tone of your day and solidifies good habits that will carry you through the rest of your life.

What makes a great morning routine?

- Early Start: It's not about waking up at 5 AM exactly, but having time in the morning where the world is still, allowing you to focus on yourself.
- No Distractions: No phone, no emails, no social media. It's about peace and focus.
- Time for Yourself: Use this time for reflection, exercise, reading, or personal development.

- A Healthy Start: Hydrate, eat something nutritious, and start with a clear, positive mindset.

What Happens When You Own Your Morning

Let's break it down: When you wake up at least an hour earlier than usual (whether at 5 AM, 6 AM, or 7 AM), you get a head start before the day's demands begin. You enter the day with intention rather than reaction.

- Mental Clarity: The early hours are the quietest of the day. There are no emails, no meetings, no distractions. This gives you the opportunity to focus entirely on your goals for the day.
- Physical Energy: By waking up early, you give your body time to energize before diving into the chaos of the world. Whether you engage in exercise or simply stretch and hydrate, your body benefits from the early focus on wellness.
- Sense of Control: Waking up early doesn't mean you have to be productive right away. You simply take the time to set the stage for your day. This sense of control builds confidence and mental strength.

Steps to Implement the 5AM Rule (Even at 7AM)

Now, let's get practical. Here's how you can start owning your mornings:

1. Gradually Adjust Your Wake-Up Time

The 5 AM wake-up time might sound extreme, especially if you're not a morning person. Start small—move your wake-up time back by 15-minute increments each day. Aim for a full adjustment after one week.

If you're starting with a 7 AM wake-up time, try setting your alarm for 6:45 AM the first day, then 6:30 AM the next, and so on.

2. Set a Bedtime that Aligns with Your Wake-Up Time

To wake up early, you need to sleep early. Try setting a consistent bedtime that gives you at least 7–8 hours of rest. Create a relaxing pre-sleep ritual, such as reading a book, dimming the lights, or practicing mindfulness, to help you wind down.

3. Create a Morning Routine That Works for You

It's crucial to build a routine that sets you up for success. Here's an example of a powerful morning routine:

- Wake up at 6 AM.
- Hydrate with a glass of water to rehydrate your body after a long night's rest.
- Exercise for 10–15 minutes—this could be stretching, yoga, a quick walk, or a light workout. Get your body moving.
- Meditate or journal for 5–10 minutes. Reflect on what you're grateful for and set your intentions for the day.
- Eat a healthy breakfast to fuel your mind and body. Avoid sugary snacks that lead to energy crashes later.
- Plan your day. Spend 5–10 minutes outlining the top 3 priorities you want to tackle, so your mind is clear and ready to go.

Overcoming Common Challenges

Even with the best intentions, waking up early can be tough. Here are some solutions to common challenges:

1. **Feeling Groggy in the Morning?**
   - Solution: Hydrate immediately after waking up. A cold glass of water helps reset your body and kick-starts your metabolism. You might also want to try light stretching or even a quick walk to shake off grogginess.
2. **The Temptation to Stay in Bed**
   - Solution: Place your alarm across the room, so you have to get out of bed to turn it off. Also, keep your phone away from your bed to avoid distractions.
3. **Struggling to Find Motivation**
   - Solution: Focus on the reward—whether it's the quiet time to yourself, the energy boost from exercise, or the productivity you're setting yourself up for. Remind yourself of the big picture goals you're working toward.

The Ripple Effect

What's remarkable about early mornings is how they positively impact other areas of your life. Starting the day on your terms creates a ripple effect of productivity, energy, and clarity throughout the day. By the time others are starting their workday, you've already accomplished something significant. You've set yourself up for success.

You've learned that focus begins early. By owning your morning, you not only get ahead of distractions but also gain a deep sense of accomplishment before the world even wakes up.

Your Task Today

- Wake up 30 minutes earlier than usual. Use that time for reflection, hydration, and setting your intentions for the day.
- Create a morning routine that you can follow every day. It doesn't need to be perfect, just consistent.
- Track how you feel after completing your morning routine. Write down how your body and mind feel differently than they do when you wake up and jump straight into the day.

Looking Ahead

You are learning how to make time your ally. You're teaching yourself that the early hours of the day are the most valuable. The more you own your mornings, the more control you'll feel over your days, your habits, and your life.

In the next chapter, we will discuss how to create a system that reduces distractions and allows you to focus on one thing at a time.

Quote to Remember:

"The early morning has gold in its mouth."

– Benjamin Franklin

CHAPTER 23
One Screen Rule

"Switching between apps is poison to your brain."

In today's world, multitasking is celebrated. We pride ourselves on the ability to juggle emails, social media, work, entertainment, and more—all at the same time. But what if I told you that this approach is actually hurting your focus? What if switching between screens and apps constantly is actually making you less efficient?

The One Screen Rule is a simple but powerful principle: You can only focus on one thing at a time. In an age where distractions are constant and multi-tasking is normalized, this rule can help you regain control over your attention, improve your productivity, and prevent burnout.

Why Switching Screens is So Harmful

Imagine you're working on a critical task, and your phone pings with a new notification. Instantly, you switch from your work to check the message. You may even try to reply, but before you know it, you find yourself scrolling through Instagram or YouTube.

Thirty minutes later, you realize you've strayed far from the original task.

This is the essence of task-switching—the constant back-and-forth between multiple apps, tabs, and tasks. Though it may seem like you're being productive, research shows that task-switching actually reduces productivity and increases mental fatigue.

Here's why:

- **Cognitive Load:** Our brains are designed to focus on one task at a time. When you switch between tasks, you are forcing your brain to jump back and forth, which increases cognitive load and decreases efficiency.
- **Attention Fragmentation:** Constantly jumping from one app or screen to another fragments your attention. You're never fully engaged with any single task, leading to shallow work and a decreased ability to retain information.
- **Loss of Flow:** The more you switch tasks, the harder it becomes to enter flow state—that deep, focused mode where you produce your best work. The One Screen Rule helps you stay in a singular zone, boosting your concentration and output.

The Neuroscience Behind It

Your brain wasn't built for multitasking, despite what society often tells you. Neuroscientific studies have shown that when you attempt to multitask, your brain doesn't actually handle two tasks at once. Instead, it rapidly shifts focus between them. This constant switching leads to something called cognitive residue, where parts of your brain are still "stuck" on previous tasks.

This is why even if you think you're handling multiple tasks, it feels like you're not getting anything done. The mental energy required for this switching drains you, which leaves you feeling exhausted by the end of the day.

The One Screen Rule: What Is It?

The One Screen Rule is straightforward: when you're working, you focus on one screen at a time. No switching between apps or tabs. If you're working on your laptop, only keep relevant tabs open. If you're on your phone, only focus on the task at hand.

Here's what this rule entails:

- **Commit to one screen at a time:** Whether it's your phone or computer, keep it simple. If you're writing an email, do just that. If you're working on a project, don't have multiple windows or apps open. Focus only on the work that matters.
- **Use focus modes:** Utilize settings on your devices like "Do Not Disturb," "Focus Mode," or "Night Shift" to eliminate distractions. These modes can silence notifications and help you maintain focus.
- **Set strict boundaries**: When you're working, set clear boundaries for yourself. No checking social media, no replying to random messages, and no answering calls unless they're urgent. Stick to one thing at a time.
- **Minimize screen clutter**: Your desktop, phone screen, or browser should reflect only the things that matter. Clear out unnecessary tabs, apps, or windows that might tempt you into switching focus.

How the One Screen Rule Boosts Your Focus

The One Screen Rule isn't just about being more productive—it's about protecting your attention and deepening your focus. By committing to this rule, you can achieve the following:

- **Improved Productivity:** When you eliminate distractions and stop task-switching, you'll find that your ability to complete tasks increases. You're no longer jumping between emails, social media, and work-related tasks, so you can dedicate all your energy to completing one thing at a time.
- **Better Quality Work:** With deeper focus on one task, the quality of your output improves. Instead of bouncing between low-focus tasks, you give your brain the time and space it needs to produce thoughtful and high-quality results.
- **Enhanced Memory and Learning:** Studies show that focusing on one thing at a time leads to better retention of information. By immersing yourself fully in a task, you absorb information in a more meaningful way, which leads to stronger memory and learning outcomes.
- **Decreased Stress and Anxiety:** Constantly switching between tasks can cause your brain to feel overwhelmed. The One Screen Rule helps reduce this stress by providing you with mental clarity and a sense of accomplishment as you focus on completing one task at a time.

How to Implement the One Screen Rule

Start with small changes in your daily routine to implement the One Screen Rule. Here's a step-by-step guide:

- **Identify Your Distractions:** Start by observing which apps or tasks distract you the most. Is it social media? Email? Games? Recognizing these distractions is the first step to minimizing them.
- **Set Priorities**: Focus on the task at hand and eliminate distractions. For example, if you're working on a project, close all unrelated apps. If you're answering emails, don't check social media or messages at the same time.
- **Limit Screen Time:** Create a schedule where you assign specific time blocks for each task. For instance, decide to only use your phone for social media for 15 minutes after your work session. This helps to curb distractions and stay on task.
- **Use Tools:** Leverage technology to your advantage. Tools like Forest, Focus Will, or Stay Focused can help limit screen time and keep you focused on one task.
- **Mindful Breaks:** After each focused session, take a brief break to recharge. Use the break time to stand up, stretch, and avoid jumping to other screens. This helps reset your mind and keeps you refreshed.

Overcoming Resistance

We know how easy it is to succumb to distractions, especially in a world of endless notifications. However, as you begin to see the benefits of focusing on one task at a time, the resistance to following the One Screen Rule will fade. Here are a few ways to overcome the temptation:

- **Awareness:** Be mindful of when you're switching screens or multitasking. Recognizing when you're doing it is the first step to stopping the cycle.

- **Accountability:** Share your goals with a friend, colleague, or mentor who can hold you accountable to sticking with the One Screen Rule.
- **Gradual Implementation**: If jumping straight into this rule feels daunting, start by limiting your screen switching for just an hour or two per day, then gradually increase the time.

Task for Today

- Identify the biggest distractions in your day that come from switching between screens or apps. Write them down.
- Set up your workspace: Clean up your computer or phone, closing unnecessary tabs, apps, or programs. Focus on what you need to do.
- Commit to one screen for the next 3 hours: Choose a task (e.g., work, studying, or creative work) and commit to focusing on that single task for a set period of time. Avoid jumping between tasks and resist the urge to switch screens.

Conclusion

The One Screen Rule is about discipline, focus, and intentionality. In a world full of distractions, this simple rule can help you regain control of your time and boost your productivity. By focusing on one task at a time and eliminating unnecessary task-switching, you create a solid foundation for achieving greater mental clarity, efficiency, and success.

Now that you've learned the importance of focusing on one task at a time, the next chapter will focus on creating a study environment that supports your goals and enhances your productivity.

Quote to Remember:

"Multitasking is a lie. Focus on one thing at a time, and you'll be amazed at what you can accomplish."

CHAPTER 24
Study With Me (Virtual Room)

"Focus grows in groups. Join others today."

In the era of digital learning and virtual environments, one concept has recently gained significant traction in the world of productivity and focus—study with me sessions. You've probably seen videos of people working or studying live on platforms like YouTube, where the atmosphere is calm, focused, and encouraging. This chapter will explore the power of studying in a group, virtually, and how the right virtual study environment can drastically enhance your ability to focus and be productive.

Why Study with Me Works

The concept of study with me sessions is deceptively simple: you join a virtual room, tune in to a live study session, and work alongside others. What could seem like a small change is actually a game-changer when it comes to improving focus and productivity. Here's why:

- **Social Accountability**: One of the most significant benefits of studying with others, even virtually, is the feeling of accountability. When you're in a virtual study room with others, even though you may not speak to them directly, there's an underlying understanding that everyone is there to work. This social pressure can often be the motivating force that helps you overcome procrastination and distractions.

- **A Shared Focused Environment**: The power of a study group isn't in the conversation—it's in the shared environment of focus. When everyone is quietly working toward their goals, the collective energy often encourages individual focus. In contrast, when you study alone in a room with your phone or other distractions, the temptation to drift away is higher. A virtual study room eliminates that distraction, reinforcing the idea of a quiet, uninterrupted space.
- **Peer Influence:** Human beings are inherently social creatures, and we are often influenced by the behaviour of others around us. If you're studying alongside others who are equally focused and working hard, you're more likely to stay on task as well. This peer influence can create a powerful positive feedback loop—seeing others work diligently makes you want to do the same.
- **Structured Time:** In a virtual study room, there is often a clear start and end time, which adds structure to your study sessions. This can create a sense of urgency that pushes you to focus more effectively. It's a way of mimicking the structure that we often lose when studying on our own, where it's easy to procrastinate or lose track of time.
- **Less Isolation:** Studying can sometimes feel like a solitary task, but being in a virtual study room helps combat this isolation. Even though you may be physically alone, you're still part of a community. This feeling of connection can make your study time feel less tedious and more enjoyable.

How to Set Up Your Own Virtual Study Room

Now that you understand why studying with others, even virtually, can be so effective, let's discuss how to set up your own virtual study room or study with me session. Setting up your environment intentionally can maximize your productivity and help you make the most out of your study time.

1. Choose the Right Platform

There are numerous platforms available that can help you set up a virtual study session. Some popular ones include:

- **Zoom:** A familiar platform for video conferencing, which allows you to create a virtual room where everyone can be on video, mute their microphones, and study together.
- **YouTube Live:** Many content creators and students host live study sessions on YouTube. You can either join these sessions or create your own channel for live streaming your study sessions.
- **Discord:** This app is primarily known for gaming, but it has become increasingly popular for study groups. You can create a study server, where members can join and use voice or text channels to stay connected while working.
- **Twitch**: Similar to YouTube, Twitch is another platform used for live streaming. Many students now use Twitch to stream their study sessions, allowing others to watch and join them in focused study time.

Choose the platform that works best for you. Consider features like the ability to mute microphones, share videos, or screen share if you need help with your study materials. The key is to find a platform that makes it easy for you and your study group to stay connected.

2. Set Clear Study Goals for the Session

Before you join a virtual study room, make sure you have a clear set of study goals. Know what you want to achieve during the session—whether it's completing a set of exercises, writing an essay, or reviewing for an exam. The more specific your goals, the easier it will be to stay focused.

Here's how you can break it down:

- **Set a Time Limit:** Decide in advance how long you will study. One hour? Two? Stick to the timeline so that you don't feel overwhelmed.
- **Outline What You Want to Accomplish**: Be clear about the tasks you want to complete during the study session. For example, "Today, I will finish chapter 4 of my history textbook and take notes on it."
- **Track Your Progress:** As you complete each task, cross it off your list. This helps create a sense of accomplishment and keeps you motivated.

3. Create an Environment That Minimizes Distractions

Even though you're studying virtually with others, the environment in which you study matters a lot. Here are a few tips to create an ideal environment for studying:

- **Declutter Your Workspace:** Just like a physical study room, your virtual study room benefits from being organized. Clear away any unnecessary tabs or programs that might distract you.

- **Use Focus Apps:** Consider using apps like Forest, Focus Will, or Stay Focused to limit your distractions while studying. These apps can block distracting websites or apps during your study time.
- **Mute Your Phone:** If you're using your phone for study-related tasks, mute notifications. Make sure that you are not constantly checking your phone for messages or social media updates.
- **Wear Headphones:** To eliminate background noise, consider using noise-cancelling headphones. This will help you stay immersed in the study session and avoid being distracted by outside noise.

4. Engage with Others in the Study Room

While the main goal is to focus, you can still engage with others in the study room, and that interaction can help you stay motivated. Here's how:

- **Use the Chat Feature:** If you're studying in a group, consider using the chat feature to discuss study materials or motivate each other.
- **Share Study Tips:** You might be surprised by the amount of useful tips and resources others can share. If you're working through a challenging concept, ask your peers for help or share a resource that might assist others.
- **Encourage Silent Breaks**: Plan for short breaks to relax and recharge. These moments of rest are just as important as the study time itself.

5. Stick to the Schedule

When studying in a virtual room, consistency is key. If you commit to studying at a specific time, stick to that schedule. Over time, this routine will become ingrained, and it will help train your brain to stay focused during these sessions. You'll also find that the more regularly you join these virtual study rooms, the more motivated you'll feel to keep coming back.

The Benefits of Virtual Study Rooms

The benefits of study groups, whether in person or virtual, are significant. But when combined with the flexibility and reach of digital platforms, the virtual study room has several unique advantages:

- **Flexibility:** You can join study groups from anywhere in the world, and at any time, without having to leave your home.
- **Diverse Perspectives:** By studying with people from different backgrounds, you can gain new insights and learn in new ways that might not have occurred to you otherwise.
- **Reduced Isolation**: Studying in a virtual group environment can help reduce the isolation often felt when studying alone, which can lead to better focus and a more enjoyable study experience.
- **Motivation:** The presence of other focused individuals, even virtually, can push you to stay on task and give your best effort.

Task for Today

- **Join a Virtual Study Session:** Find a study group or create your own on a platform like Zoom, YouTube Live, or Discord. Set a goal for the session and commit to focusing only on your work for a set time.

- **Set Up Your Study Space:** Prepare your workspace by eliminating distractions. Close unnecessary apps, mute notifications, and ensure your environment is conducive to studying.
- **Track Your Focus:** During the session, note how long you stayed focused without switching tasks. Reflect on how the group dynamic impacted your concentration.

Quote to Remember:

"Focus grows in groups. When you work together, your attention multiplies."

CHAPTER 25
Reward Yourself Right

"Celebrate victories, not distractions."

In our fast-paced, results-oriented world, it's easy to get caught up in the grind and forget to celebrate the small wins. For many, the focus tends to be on the end goal—graduating, landing the perfect job, or completing a big project. However, it's the small victories that truly drive long-term progress. The rewards you give yourself for achieving these smaller milestones not only provide motivation but also serve as a reinforcement tool to keep you moving toward your bigger goals.

In this chapter, we'll explore the power of rewards and how to use them effectively to reinforce positive habits and maintain focus throughout your journey. Rewarding yourself right isn't about indulging in distractions; it's about recognizing and celebrating consistent progress and creating a system that ensures you stay on track.

Why Rewards Matter

Rewards are a powerful tool in behaviour change, motivation, and habit formation. Our brains are wired to seek pleasure, and when we successfully complete a task, our brain releases dopamine, the "feel-good" chemical that reinforces the behaviour. Dopamine acts as a positive reinforcement, making us want to repeat the behaviour again in the future. By rewarding ourselves strategically, we can train our brains to associate hard work and focus with positive outcomes, increasing the likelihood of sustained productivity and attention.

The act of rewarding yourself for completing a task or reaching a goal is more than just a way to feel good in the moment. It's also about creating a positive feedback loop that motivates you to keep striving for more. Over time, this approach will enhance your ability to stay focused, improve your productivity, and ultimately create lasting habits that contribute to success.

However, it's important to distinguish between rewarding your efforts and rewarding distractions. In today's world, it's easy to fall into the trap of rewarding ourselves with unhealthy distractions, such as mindlessly scrolling through social media or binge-watching videos. These types of rewards may provide temporary pleasure but offer no long-term benefits and can even worsen the very distractions you're trying to overcome.

The key is to focus on rewards that align with your goals—rewards that help to reinforce the positive habits you're working hard to build.

The Right Way to Reward Yourself

Rewarding yourself effectively doesn't mean simply indulging in any form of gratification. Instead, it involves choosing rewards that motivate and energize you in ways that contribute to your growth. Here are some guidelines to ensure you're rewarding yourself the right way:

1. Align Rewards with Your Progress

Rewards should match the effort or progress you've made. For example, after a long, focused study session, treat yourself to a reward that enhances your well-being, such as taking a walk, reading a chapter of a book you enjoy, or having a healthy snack. If you've completed a significant milestone, you could reward yourself with something larger—perhaps a weekend activity you've been wanting to do or taking time to engage in a hobby.

This ensures that the rewards you give yourself are not just indulgences but are aligned with the values and habits you're trying to develop.

2. Choose Rewards that Rejuvenate You

Rewards should leave you feeling recharged and motivated to keep going, not drained or demotivated. If you reward yourself with activities that don't support your long-term goals, you risk undoing the progress you've made. For example, indulging in mindless scrolling on social media or watching TV for hours might feel good in the short term, but it's unlikely to energize you or help you continue making progress.

Instead, choose rewards that help you recharge your focus. Taking a short walk outside, meditating, enjoying a favourite hobby, or spending quality time with family or friends can refresh your mind and body, helping you return to your tasks with renewed energy.

3. Reward Progress, Not Perfection

Many people make the mistake of only rewarding themselves when they achieve perfection. But focusing solely on big, perfect outcomes can create unnecessary pressure and stress. The journey is just as important as the destination. Celebrate incremental progress, whether it's finishing a chapter, sticking to your focus plan for the day, or even just improving your concentration.

This helps to avoid burnout and creates a growth mindset, where small steps forward are acknowledged and appreciated. It also reinforces the belief that even minor achievements are worth celebrating, which boosts motivation.

4. Be Mindful of How Often You Reward Yourself

It's important to find a balance in how frequently you reward yourself. If you reward yourself too often, the rewards lose their power, and they no longer serve as a motivation tool. On the other hand, if you reward yourself too infrequently, you risk feeling deprived and demotivated.

Create a reward system based on the significance of the task at hand. For example:

- **Short tasks** (like completing a focused study session): Reward yourself with a small break, a healthy snack, or a short relaxation activity.
- **Medium tasks** (like completing a chapter or finishing a project): Treat yourself to a favourite activity, a meal at a restaurant, or a quick getaway.
- **Big milestones** (like achieving a long-term goal or completing a large project): Celebrate with a larger

reward, like a weekend trip, a day off, or a special purchase.

5. Enjoy the Process

The most powerful reward is the satisfaction and enjoyment you feel from the process itself. Sometimes, the most fulfilling reward is simply the pleasure of knowing that you've worked hard, stayed focused, and made progress toward your goals. This intrinsic sense of accomplishment is often more rewarding than external rewards.

It's important to acknowledge that enjoying the journey itself is a reward that reinforces your commitment to your goals. Celebrate the feeling of progress, even before reaching the final destination.

How to Implement a Reward System in Your Life

To effectively implement a reward system, it's essential to have a plan. Below are some steps to help you build a reward system that will motivate you and reinforce your focus and productivity:

- **Set Clear Goals**: Define your short-term and long-term goals clearly. This helps you identify when it's time to reward yourself and ensures that you're focusing on the right tasks.
- **Choose Meaningful Rewards**: Take the time to choose rewards that truly motivate and energize you. Ensure that your rewards align with your values and support your long-term objectives.
- **Track Progress:** Keep a record of your tasks and progress. This will make it easier to identify when you've hit a milestone and deserve a reward. Use a journal, an app, or a simple checklist to stay on top of your goals.

- **Reflect Regularly:** As you work through your tasks, regularly reflect on your progress. Recognize the effort you're putting in and the rewards you've earned. This helps you stay focused and ensures you don't miss out on celebrating your achievements.
- **Don't Overdo It:** While rewards are essential, it's important to avoid using them excessively. If you reward yourself too often, it diminishes the value of the reward and reduces its effectiveness. Reserve rewards for meaningful milestones.

Task for Today

- Create Your Reward System: Take a moment to write down your current goals. For each goal, define an appropriate reward system. Decide what you will reward yourself with for small, medium, and large achievements.
- Enjoy Your Rewards: Choose a task you've been procrastinating on, and once you complete it, reward yourself as planned. Enjoy the process of completing the task and acknowledge the satisfaction it brings.
- Track Your Progress: Keep track of your rewards and reflect on how they make you feel. Does the reward energize you to stay focused? Is there a particular reward that feels especially motivating?

Quote to Remember:

"Success is the sum of small efforts, repeated day in and day out. Celebrate the little wins, for they lead to bigger victories."

CHAPTER 26
Phone Lock Mode

"Set rules your future self will thank you for."

In the modern world, our phones are both our greatest tool and our biggest distraction. They connect us to the world, give us access to a wealth of information, and enable us to communicate effortlessly. However, the very thing that makes our phones so powerful is also what makes them so dangerous to our focus and productivity. Social media apps, constant notifications, and mindless scrolling can drain our time, attention, and energy. That's where Phone Lock Mode comes in.

Phone Lock Mode is a practice that allows you to take control of your phone and ensure it works for you, rather than against you. It's a tool that helps you create boundaries around your phone usage, reduce distractions, and maintain focus on what matters most. By setting up Phone Lock Mode, you create an environment that supports your goals, encourages productivity, and helps you regain control of your time and attention.

In this chapter, we'll dive into the importance of setting boundaries with your phone, how to activate and use Phone Lock

Mode, and how this strategy can help you stay focused and achieve your goals. It's time to stop letting your phone dictate your day and start using it as a tool that serves you.

The Need for Phone Lock Mode

Before diving into the setup process, it's important to understand why Phone Lock Mode is essential. Our phones are designed to capture our attention. Every app, every notification, and every alert is engineered to keep us hooked. Unfortunately, this constant stimulation can make it incredibly difficult to focus on tasks that require sustained attention, such as studying, working, or even engaging in personal development activities.

Here are some key reasons why Phone Lock Mode is necessary:

1. Constant Notifications are Distracting

Notifications are a key reason why our phones are so distracting. Whether it's an Instagram like, a new WhatsApp message, or a Facebook notification, these constant interruptions break our concentration and make it difficult to stay focused. Even the mere act of checking your phone for a notification can pull you out of a productive state and set you back.

2. Social media is a Time Sink

The allure of social media is hard to resist. Whether you're scrolling through your feed, watching the latest YouTube video, or replying to a message, the endless stream of content can easily become a time sink. Research shows that people can spend hours a day on their phones, with much of that time spent mindlessly scrolling or checking notifications. This not only wastes time but also leads to lower levels of focus and productivity.

3. Smartphones Can Trigger Procrastination

For many people, the phone serves as a procrastination tool. Instead of tackling important tasks, you may find yourself picking up your phone and scrolling through social media or playing games to avoid work. This creates a cycle of procrastination, where you spend hours avoiding the very thing you should be focusing on.

4. It's Easy to Lose Track of Time

The ease with which we can spend time on our phones means that we often lose track of time. A 5-minute break to check your phone can easily turn into 30 minutes of wasted time. Without structure and boundaries, your phone can easily hijack your day.

Setting Up Phone Lock Mode

Now that we understand why Phone Lock Mode is so essential, it's time to set it up. The goal of this strategy is to create time blocks where your phone is either fully locked down or restricted to only essential apps. By creating clear boundaries around your phone usage, you free up mental space to focus on more important tasks.

1. Use Built-In Screen Time or Focus Features

Most smartphones come with built-in features designed to limit screen time and reduce distractions. These tools can help you set up Phone Lock Mode effectively.

- **iPhone:** The Screen Time feature on iPhones allows you to set limits on app usage, schedule downtime, and track how much time you spend on each app. You can set time limits for specific apps and enable Do Not Disturb during focused work hours.

- **Android:** Android phones have a Digital Wellbeing feature, which provides similar functionality. You can set app timers, create focus modes, and even schedule downtime when you'll be unable to use your phone.

2. Activate Focus Mode (or Do Not Disturb)

Focus Mode, also known as Do Not Disturb, is a great feature that helps you block out unnecessary distractions while you work. When you activate Focus Mode, you can choose which apps or notifications you still want to receive and mute the rest. This allows you to stay connected to essential communication while cutting off the noise from apps like social media, news, or gaming.

Here's how to set it up:

- On iPhone: Go to Settings > Focus > Do Not Disturb and customize which apps or people can send notifications during work hours.
- On Android: Go to Settings > Digital Wellbeing > Focus Mode and select the apps you want to block temporarily.

3. Set App Limits

App limits are a great way to restrict your usage of certain apps that tend to steal your attention. Whether it's social media, games, or video streaming apps, limiting their usage helps prevent mindless scrolling and ensures that you stay on task.

Set limits for specific apps or categories of apps. For example:

- Social media: Limit apps like Instagram, Twitter, or Facebook to 30 minutes per day.
- Games: Set limits for gaming apps like PUBG or Candy Crush to avoid losing hours in front of your screen.
- Video Streaming: Restrict video apps to an hour per day to avoid binge-watching.

4. Lock the Phone Completely

If you're serious about staying focused, consider locking your phone completely during designated focus times. You can do this manually by setting up downtime in your phone's settings, where you cannot access certain apps or even unlock the phone without a password.

Additionally, you can use third-party apps like Forest, Focus Will, or AppLocker, which lock your phone or specific apps for a set amount of time, keeping you from using it as a distraction.

5. Create a Tech-Free Zone

In addition to using phone lock features, create a tech-free zone in your daily routine. For example, make it a rule not to use your phone during meals, while studying, or in bed before sleep. This helps to ensure that your phone doesn't interrupt important moments of the day.

Benefits of Phone Lock Mode

When you activate Phone Lock Mode, you'll experience a number of positive changes in your focus and productivity:

- **Increased Focus**: By blocking distractions, you'll be able to stay focused on your tasks for longer periods of time.

- **Better Time Management**: You'll be more aware of how much time you're spending on your phone, allowing you to allocate time for important tasks more efficiently.
- **Reduced Stress:** Constant notifications and interruptions create a sense of urgency and stress. Phone Lock Mode reduces this mental clutter.
- **Improved Mental Clarity**: By limiting distractions, you create more mental space for deep thinking, creativity, and problem-solving.
- **Better Sleep**: By reducing screen time, especially before bed, you'll improve your sleep quality and feel more rested in the morning.

Task for Today

- **Activate Phone Lock Mode:** Set up Focus Mode or Do Not Disturb on your phone. Choose one or two apps to limit and schedule a downtime session where your phone is fully locked.
- **Designate a Tech-Free Zone:** Identify a space in your day (mealtimes, study time, or before bed) where you'll commit to not using your phone.
- **Track Your Progress**: For the next few days, track how well you stick to your Phone Lock Mode and reflect on how it impacts your focus and productivity.

CHAPTER 27
1% Daily Growth

"You don't need motivation. You need micro progress."

In the pursuit of achieving big goals, many people make the mistake of thinking that they need huge bursts of energy, motivation, or massive leaps forward to see meaningful results. We often find ourselves setting grand New Year's resolutions or making big, bold promises, thinking that these sweeping gestures will propel us to success. However, the reality is different. Success is built on small, consistent improvements that compound over time. This is where the concept of 1% Daily Growth comes in.

In this chapter, we'll explore how focusing on small, incremental improvements every day can lead to massive transformation over time. By adopting the mindset of micro progress, we shift our focus away from the overwhelming task of changing everything at once and instead embrace the idea that small changes, when compounded, lead to exponential growth. Whether it's in your study habits, health, or personal development, small, consistent steps taken every day will ultimately lead you to success.

Let's dive into the concept of 1% Daily Growth, why it works, and how you can start applying it to your life right now.

The Power of Consistency

The key to achieving any long-term goal lies in consistency. It's not the occasional bursts of effort or occasional big wins that lead to success—it's the daily commitment to making small improvements, even if they seem insignificant at the time.

Think about this: if you were to improve by just 1% every day, in a year, you would have improved by 365%. That's a remarkable change, and it's a result of consistently choosing to make small progress. Conversely, if you got 1% worse every day, by the end of the year, you'd be 37% worse off. This simple mathematical principle shows the immense power of compound growth.

By focusing on 1% daily growth, you reduce the pressure of perfection and instead focus on gradual progress. This is an approach that encourages continuous learning, experimentation, and improvement, no matter how small the changes may seem.

Why 1%?

The concept of 1% might seem too small to make a difference. However, small changes add up in ways that are difficult to appreciate in the short term. It's easy to underestimate the significance of tiny actions, but over time, they create momentum and lead to profound results.

Here's why 1% is so powerful:

- **It's Manageable**: Making a 1% improvement is doable. It's not overwhelming or intimidating. You don't need to completely overhaul your life or start from scratch—just commit to making tiny changes each day.

- **It's Sustainable:** Small improvements don't require excessive effort or willpower. They can be sustained over time, which is essential for long-term success. Unlike drastic changes, which often lead to burnout or regression, incremental progress is sustainable and can become a habit.
- **It Builds Momentum:** Small improvements lead to momentum. As you start to see small wins, you'll feel more motivated to keep going, and this cycle of success reinforces itself. Over time, the growth becomes exponential as your efforts compound.
- **It Creates Consistency**: The 1% principle is about creating daily habits that you can maintain. It's not about being perfect but about showing up consistently. This daily practice allows you to develop the skills, knowledge, and discipline needed to achieve your long-term goals.
- **It Minimizes Pressure:** When you commit to improving by just 1% per day, you take off the pressure to achieve big results immediately. This approach focuses on progress, not perfection, which makes the journey less stressful and more enjoyable.

How to Apply 1% Daily Growth to Your Life

Now that you understand the power of 1% daily growth, the next step is to incorporate this mindset into your daily life. Here's how you can get started:

1. Set Specific, Measurable Goals

Instead of setting vague or lofty goals, break them down into specific and measurable actions. For example:

- If your goal is to improve your focus, you can aim to increase your focused study time by 1% each day.
- If you want to improve your health, you could commit to adding 1% more vegetables to your diet each day.
- If you want to learn a new skill, you can dedicate just 1% more time to practicing that skill every day.

2. Track Your Progress

Tracking is crucial to ensure that you're on the right path. Whether you use a journal, an app, or a spreadsheet, make sure you're keeping track of your daily growth. By seeing the incremental changes you're making, you'll stay motivated and be able to measure your success over time.

3. Focus on Small Habits

The key to 1% daily growth is focusing on small, actionable habits that you can implement every day. For instance:

- Study: If you study for an hour today, increase your study time by 1% tomorrow. This could be as small as adding an extra minute or two to your study time each day.
- Exercise: If you work out for 20 minutes today, add a minute or two tomorrow. Gradually increase your time or intensity, making small adjustments each day.
- Reading: If you read 10 pages of a book today, read 11 pages tomorrow. Incremental increases in your reading habits will lead to substantial growth over time.

4. Celebrate Small Wins

One of the most important aspects of 1% daily growth is celebrating your small wins. Every time you make progress, no matter how small, take a moment to appreciate your efforts. This positive reinforcement boosts motivation and encourages you to keep going.

5. Be Patient

Remember that success is not immediate. The process of making small improvements can feel slow, but don't be discouraged. Over time, these small steps will compound, and the results will become visible. Be patient with yourself and trust the process.

The Compound Effect: Small Changes, Big Results

The real power of 1% daily growth lies in the compound effect. When you make small, consistent improvements, those changes build on each other. Each day's 1% improvement is not isolated—it adds to the progress made the day before, creating a snowball effect.

For example, if you consistently improve by just 1% every day, here's how your growth will look after a few months:

- After 30 days, you will have improved by 30%.
- After 90 days, you will have improved by 90%.
- After a year, you will have improved by 365%, a significant transformation from where you started.

This exponential growth is why the 1% strategy is so powerful. It's the compound effect in action: tiny, consistent changes lead to massive, long-term success.

Task for Today

- Identify One Area for 1% Improvement: Choose one area of your life (study, health, work, or personal development) where you can make a small improvement each day. Write it down.
- Track Your Progress: Start tracking your progress each day. Note the small changes you're making and celebrate each win, no matter how small.
- Commit to the Process: Understand that success comes through consistency. Commit to making 1% progress every day and trust that the results will compound over time.

Quote to Remember:

"*Success is the sum of small efforts, repeated day in and day out.*"

CHAPTER 28
Focus for Life Blueprint

"From 30 days to 3000 days."

After completing your 30-day Focus Reset, you're no longer just someone who occasionally focuses well—you've developed the ability to sustain focus over long periods. However, as we've learned, achieving lasting results doesn't stop after 30 days. It's about embedding these habits into the fabric of your life. Focus isn't just something you practice temporarily; it's something you integrate into your lifestyle.

In this chapter, we'll create your Focus for Life Blueprint—a plan for transforming the powerful lessons you've learned during the 30-day challenge into long-term habits and practices. You will now begin to structure your life for sustained focus and productivity over the next 90 days and beyond, setting you up for a life of continued growth and success.

Step 1: Visualize Your Future Self

Before diving into the practical strategies that will create your focus-cantered lifestyle, take a moment to reflect on who you want to become. Focus is not just about getting things done in the short term—it's about becoming the kind of person who consistently produces results in all areas of life.

Think about your future self. Imagine a version of you who wakes up every day with purpose, clear goals, and laser-like focus on the things that matter. This version of yourself doesn't get distracted easily, doesn't procrastinate, and has the mental strength to follow through on commitments. How does that person behave? What does their day look like? What are they proud of?

Visualization is a powerful tool because it allows you to picture your ideal future self and see where you want to go. It builds motivation and sets a clear vision. This version of yourself is already inside you, waiting to be brought to life through consistency and daily practice.

Step 2: Structure Your Days Around Focus

Now that you have a vision for your future self, it's time to structure your daily routine to ensure that you're living in alignment with that vision. Focus needs time, space, and consistency to thrive. Without a clear plan, you'll quickly find yourself slipping back into old habits. Here's how to structure your day for maximum focus:

1. Start with the Morning Routine

Your morning routine sets the tone for the day. The first few hours after you wake up are the most critical, as they determine whether you'll feel in control or overwhelmed for the rest of the day. To optimize your morning:

- **Wake up early:** Try to wake up at the same time every day. Aim for 5 AM or 6 AM, depending on your lifestyle, so that you have uninterrupted time to focus on yourself before the world wakes up.

- **Avoid your phone:** Don't reach for your phone as soon as you wake up. Instead, start with self-care activities like drinking water, stretching, journaling, or reading something motivational.
- **Set your intentions**: Spend 5 minutes deciding what your most important tasks are for the day. This practice gives you a sense of purpose and direction.

2. Prioritize Deep Work

Block out specific periods in your day for deep, focused work—time when you're not distracted by emails, social media, or other people. Treat this time as sacred and non-negotiable. Here's how:

- Use the Pomodoro Technique: Break your work into 25-minute intervals (Pomodoro's), with 5-minute breaks in between. After four Pomodoro's, take a longer break.
- Tackle your hardest tasks first: When your brain is fresh in the morning, dive straight into your most challenging tasks.

3. Plan Your Rest and Recovery

Focus is draining. If you don't take time to rest and recharge, you'll experience mental burnout. Integrating rest periods into your day is essential for maintaining long-term focus and productivity. Make sure to:

- Take short breaks every 25 minutes, as mentioned in the Pomodoro Technique.

- Use longer breaks strategically: Eat lunch away from your desk and spend time outside for fresh air and mental rejuvenation.
- Sleep well: Make sleep a non-negotiable priority. Aim for 7-9 hours per night of uninterrupted, high-quality sleep to fuel your brain for the next day.

4. Eliminate Distractions

One of the core elements of your Focus for Life Blueprint is creating an environment that minimizes distractions. Review your physical and digital spaces to ensure they support deep work:

- Declutter your workspace: Keep only essential items on your desk. A clean, organized space fosters clarity and focus.
- Digital Detox: Keep your phone in a different room or on airplane mode during deep work sessions. Use app blockers or Focus Mode to limit distractions.

5. End Your Day with Reflection

At the end of the day, take time to reflect on what you accomplished and how you can improve tomorrow. This is your opportunity to stay accountable to your goals and learn from your mistakes. A simple evening routine could include:

- Journaling: Write down what went well, what didn't, and what you'll do differently tomorrow.
- Track progress: Note the key tasks you completed and how much time you spent on deep work.

Step 3: Set Long-Term Goals (90-Day Focus Plan)

While your daily routine will keep you on track, it's crucial to have long-term goals to direct your focus. Your goals give you something to strive for and provide a sense of purpose in everything you do.

Here's how to create your 90-day Focus Plan:

1. Define Your Big Goals

What do you want to achieve in the next three months? These could be personal, academic, or professional goals. Some examples could be:

- Personal Growth: Reading 3 books on a subject you're passionate about.
- Academic Focus: Completing a major project or preparing for an exam.
- Career: Reaching a significant milestone at work or starting a new project.

2. Break Goals into Milestones

Now, break down these big goals into smaller, manageable tasks. Focus on what you need to do each month and week to make progress. This will prevent you from feeling overwhelmed and keep your focus aligned with your larger vision.

3. Create Weekly Check-ins

To stay accountable, schedule a weekly check-in with yourself to review your progress. Each week, assess what you've accomplished, what needs improvement, and adjust your approach for the upcoming week. This practice will keep you on track for long-term success.

Step 4: Review and Adjust Regularly

Focus isn't something you can perfect overnight, and life will inevitably present new challenges and distractions. That's why it's essential to review and adjust your plan regularly. Every 30 days, take a step back and assess how your 90-day plan is unfolding. Is it working? Do you need to tweak anything?

You might discover that your goals have shifted, or that your methods need refining. Don't be afraid to make changes—flexibility is key. The point is to stay on course and never lose sight of your bigger vision.

Conclusion: Focus for Life

Creating a Focus for Life Blueprint isn't a one-time task—it's a continuous process. The journey of building long-term focus is about making small, consistent improvements and adjusting as you go. This blueprint will serve as the framework for the rest of your life, keeping you grounded in your purpose and helping you prioritize the things that matter most.

By now, you've learned how to regain your focus, develop daily habits that support it, and create a sustainable focus system that will carry you forward into your future. But the work doesn't stop here—it's about maintaining this focus for the rest of your life.

Task for Today:

- Create your 90-day Focus Plan by defining your long-term goals and breaking them down into manageable tasks.

- Set up a weekly reflection system to monitor your progress.
- Visualize your future self and write a letter to yourself from that future perspective, celebrating all the growth and achievements you've accomplished.

Quote to Remember:

"Focus is the ability to give your full attention to one thing for an extended period, while eliminating distractions. The true power of focus lies in its consistency."

CHAPTER 29
Your Final Test

"Today, go distraction-free for 4 hours in total."

After weeks of effort, dedication, and practice, you've arrived at the final chapter of your Focus for Life journey. You've refined your ability to focus, built consistent habits, and reshaped your daily routines. But before you can truly lock in your new habits, there's one final test: testing the true strength of your focus.

This chapter is all about putting your skills to the test, and not just for an hour, but for four hours in total. This is not about just making it through a couple of minutes of deep work. This is about proving to yourself that your new focus habits are ingrained in your life, and that you have the ability to control your attention for an extended period without distractions.

Why a 4-Hour Focus Test?

You've already practiced focusing for shorter bursts. But can you sustain that focus for a longer period? The 4-hour focus test will push you to prove that your new habits can withstand longer periods of deep, undistracted work. It's a confidence-building challenge and the perfect opportunity to check how well you've internalized everything you've learned in this course.

The goal isn't to push yourself to the brink of burnout. It's about showing yourself that you can go deep into a project, task, or area of interest, and hold your attention on it for four hours. This will be a test of your willpower, but more importantly, it will highlight the changes you've made to your attention span, discipline, and productivity.

By now, you've developed strategies for focusing, and you've learned how to eliminate distractions. So this final test is really about proving that all of your hard work has paid off. You'll be able to see the growth you've made over the past 30 days and recognize how much you've improved in terms of mental strength, attention, and the ability to resist distractions.

The Final Test: What to Do

Your goal for today is to spend 4 hours in total, broken down into two or more chunks, where you focus entirely on one task, without distraction, for 45-minute periods at a time. This is your opportunity to practice sustained attention.

Here's the breakdown of how to approach the test:

1. Preparation:

Before you begin, prepare your space:

- **Declutter your workspace:** Make sure your environment is free from distractions. Clear off your desk and remove anything unnecessary.

- **Set your phone aside:** Put your phone on airplane mode, or keep it in a different room entirely. You won't need it for the next few hours.
- **Make sure you have everything you need**: Gather any materials, documents, or tools required for your task. You won't want to break your focus to look for something.

2. Break the 4 Hours into Focus Sessions:

It's likely that you won't be able to maintain perfect focus for four continuous hours. That's okay! The goal is to break this time into manageable chunks. Here's how you can do it:

- **Work in 45-minute sprints:** Work for 45 minutes, followed by a 15-minute break. After 2-3 sprints, take a longer break of 30 minutes.
- **No multitasking:** During each sprint, focus on only one task. Whether you're writing, studying, or working, dedicate that entire 45 minutes to it. Multitasking will only dilute your focus.

3. Track Your Focus and Distractions:

During your 45-minute sessions, it's important to track your focus. Here's how:

- **Record any distractions:** Whenever you feel distracted, jot down what pulled you away. Did you think about your phone? Did your mind wander? This self-awareness is key in identifying the distractions that still challenge you.
- **Stay honest**: If you're tempted to check something or take a break early, pause and remind yourself that this is a test. Stay true to the process and resist the urge.

4. Full Engagement:

Your focus isn't just about sitting still or staring at your work. You need to engage deeply with whatever task you're doing. Whether it's studying, writing, or problem-solving, bring all of your attention to it. Active engagement is key to deep focus.

How to Overcome Challenges During the Test

It's likely that you'll encounter obstacles as you work through your 4-hour test. Distractions, fatigue, and self-doubt might try to creep in. Here's how to overcome those challenges:

1. Distractions:

It's easy to get distracted, especially after a few minutes of intense focus. If you feel the urge to look at your phone, check social media, or think about something else, remind yourself of the value of staying present in the moment. Resist the temptation. Think about your long-term goals and the person you want to become.

2. Fatigue:

Sustained focus can be mentally draining. If you feel tired, take a short break, stretch, and hydrate. Sometimes, even just standing up for a moment or taking a few deep breaths can rejuvenate your mind.

3. Self-Doubt:

During the test, you may start to doubt your ability to stay focused. That's completely normal. Just keep pushing forward. The biggest barrier to overcoming distractions is persistence. Even if your mind starts to wander, gently guide it back to the task at hand.

Reflecting on the Test: What You'll Learn

At the end of the 4 hours, take a moment to reflect on the experience. Ask yourself:

- **What went well?** What tasks did you complete with full attention? How did it feel to work deeply for an extended period of time?
- **Where did you struggle?** Which distractions were hardest to overcome? Did you face any mental barriers that made focusing difficult?
- **How did your body and mind feel?** Did you experience mental fatigue? Or did you feel energized and accomplished after the challenge?

This reflection will help you identify your strengths and areas for growth. You may notice that you're more focused than you thought or that certain distractions still have a strong pull. Use this information to improve your strategies and fine-tune your focus habits for the future.

Post-Test: Locking In Your Focus for Life

Congratulations! Completing the 4-hour focus test is a major milestone in your focus journey. This test is more than just a challenge; it's a symbol of how far you've come. Your next step is to make this new focus lifestyle permanent.

After completing the test, you've shown yourself that you can focus for extended periods, and now it's time to lock in this habit for life. Here's how to do that:

- Integrate these long focus sessions into your daily routine: As you move forward, make deep, distraction-free work a part of your everyday life.
- Review and refine: Each month, revisit your focus strategies. Identify areas that still need work and refine your methods.
- Keep pushing your limits: As you grow more comfortable with sustained focus, increase the challenge. Start aiming for longer focus periods, like 5 or 6 hours, or even tackle multiple tasks in one extended focus block.

Conclusion

The final test was not only about seeing how well you could focus for 4 hours. It was a test of how much you've grown, how strong your mental discipline has become, and whether you've developed a lifestyle of focus.

Now, it's time to carry this newfound focus into your daily life. You've built powerful habits, you've completed this challenge, and most importantly, you've proven to yourself that focus is not just something you practice temporarily, but something you live with every day.

Task for Today:

- Take the 4-hour Focus Test.
- Reflect on what went well and where you struggled.
- Write down your key learnings and adjustments for future focus sessions.

CHAPTER 30
Graduation Day: The Focused You

"You've completed the reset. Now let's lock it in forever."

After 30 days of intentional effort, self-discipline, and practice, you've reached the final day of your Focus for Life journey. Today isn't just about concluding a course or finishing a task—it's about celebrating a transformation. A transformation that's led you to discover a new version of yourself: a version of you that is more focused, disciplined, and capable of achieving great things.

This chapter is about celebrating the journey, reflecting on the growth you've made, and locking in the focus habits you've developed so that they become permanent in your life. You've put in the work, and now it's time to acknowledge how far you've come.

Reflection on Your Growth

Take a moment to look back on how much you've changed over the past 30 days. This isn't just about achieving short-term results; it's about the long-term shifts you've made in your mindset and habits.

When you began this journey, you may have felt overwhelmed by distractions, lacked the ability to focus for extended periods, or struggled with staying consistent. But now, after completing the various exercises and tests, you've acquired the tools to take control of your attention, and you've practiced using those tools day after day. You've built a solid foundation for long-term focus.

Here's a quick reflection to help you measure your growth:

- **Focus Score Comparison:** Think back to your Focus Assessment from Day 2. What did your score look like then? What does it look like now? Has your ability to focus improved?
- **Distractions**: What distractions were most challenging for you when you began this journey? How many of them still affect you today? Have you developed strategies to handle them?
- **Productivity:** How much more productive have you become since Day 1? What results or milestones have you achieved during this 30-day focus reset?

Celebrate Your Success

This day is not just about reflection—it's about celebrating your success. You've committed yourself to something difficult for a month, and you've made a real change. Here's how to celebrate:

- **Acknowledge Your Wins**: Write down the victories, both big and small, that you've achieved over the past month. Whether it's completing tasks more efficiently, eliminating distractions, or simply feeling more in control of your time, these wins deserve to be recognized.

- **Reward Yourself**: Give yourself a well-earned reward. It could be a day of rest, a favorite treat, or even an experience that you've been putting off. Whatever it is, make sure it's something that celebrates your commitment and hard work.

- **Share Your Journey:** Celebrate with others! Share your experience with a friend, family member, or group. Tell them about the changes you've made and how you feel about your journey. This reinforces your success and helps others see the value of focus in their own lives.

Locking in Your Focus Habits for Life

While today is about celebrating your success, it's also about ensuring that this new level of focus doesn't fade away. It's essential to make these habits permanent. The good news is that you've already laid the groundwork. Now, it's time to lock them in.

Here are some strategies for making your focus habits stick:

- **Consistency Over Perfection:** Focus isn't something you achieve once and forget about. It's something you keep refining. Make focus a part of your daily routine, and don't worry about being perfect. The key is consistency. Even when distractions tempt you, commit to getting back on track.

- **Daily Rituals**: The routines you've established over the past 30 days are powerful. Keep your morning setup, study rituals, and focus sprints in place. These rituals create an environment where focus thrives, and when you continue to follow them, your focus becomes stronger and more natural.

- **Review and Adjust:** Focus isn't a static goal. It's a dynamic process. Every few weeks, review your progress. What's working well? What's still challenging? Adjust your strategies accordingly. This will help you maintain a high level of focus over time.
- **Set Long-Term Goals:** Focus isn't just for a month. It's a skill you'll carry with you for the rest of your life. Set long-term focus goals for the next 3, 6, and 12 months. Whether it's completing a large project, studying for exams, or learning a new skill, use your focus as the driving force that propels you forward.
- **Accountability**: Continue to hold yourself accountable. Track your progress, and share your goals with others who will support you in staying focused. Accountability not only reinforces your commitment, but it also helps you stay consistent over time.
- **Focus in Small Doses:** Sometimes, it's easy to lose focus if you try to do too much at once. Keep focusing in small, bite-sized doses. Even if it's only 20 minutes a day, regular focus is far more powerful than occasional bursts of long focus. Gradually increase the time as you build stamina.

Your Focus Plan for the Next 90 Days

To solidify your focus and continue to grow, it's important to have a Focus Plan for the next 90 days. This plan should outline how you're going to maintain the habits and principles you've learned.

Here's a simple framework to help you craft your plan:

- **Set Specific Goals:** What do you want to achieve in the next 90 days? Be specific. Whether it's improving your grades, completing a personal project, or improving your career skills, your focus should be aligned with clear and measurable goals.
- **Daily Focus Time**: Commit to at least 30 minutes to 1 hour of deep work every day. This could be studying, working on a passion project, or practicing a skill. The key is to ensure that every day, you're dedicating time to uninterrupted focus.
- **Checkpoints:** At the end of every week or month, review your progress. What's working? What do you need to adjust? These checkpoints will help you stay on track and make any necessary adjustments.
- **Reward System**: Build in rewards to celebrate your progress. Every week, month, or quarter, reward yourself for staying focused and achieving your goals. This will help reinforce the habit of focus.

Take the Final Focus Test

As a final step in this chapter, take the Focus Test you completed on Day 2. Compare your scores and performance. How much have you improved? Celebrate the progress you've made. Even if your score is still not perfect, be proud of how far you've come.

Congratulations, Focused You

Today, you graduate. But this isn't just a course completion; this is a life transformation. You've taken the first steps toward building a lifestyle where focus is central, and you've proven to yourself that you can change your habits for the better.

As you continue on your journey, remember this: focus is a lifelong skill. You will always need it, whether it's for personal growth, career success, or achieving your dreams. Today marks the beginning of a focused life—a life where distractions no longer control you, and where your attention is one of your greatest strengths.

Task for Today:

- Take the final focus test again and compare it to your Day 2 results.
- Write about how your habits, mindset, and ability to focus have changed over the last 30 days.
- Celebrate your graduation day with a meaningful reward.

Next Step

The journey doesn't stop here. Keep your focus strong, and use it to create the life you've always dreamed of.

Summary of the 30-Day Focus Journey

This 30-day journey is designed to help you break free from distractions, establish lasting habits of focus, and unlock your potential for productivity and growth. Through a carefully structured approach, each chapter offers powerful insights, actionable tasks, and reflection exercises aimed at reshaping your mindset and habits. Here's a comprehensive summary of the key chapters:

Week 1: Identifying and Addressing Distractions

1. **Chapter 1: The Real Enemy: Distraction**

   - The battle with distraction is internal, not external. The first step is to identify your distractions and understand their root causes.

   Task: Write down your top 3 daily distractions.

2. **Chapter 2: Your Focus Score**

   - To improve, you first need a baseline. Assess your current level of focus to track progress.

     Task: Take a Focus Assessment to measure your current focus ability.

3. **Chapter 3: Apps That Are Killing You**

    - Digital distractions, especially social media and gaming apps, are major culprits. The key is to pause or remove the most distracting apps from your phone. Task: Uninstall or pause your top 3 distracting apps.

4. **Chapter 4: Dopamine Detox Explained**

    - Dopamine, the "pleasure chemical," can hijack your brain's reward system. A detox helps reset your brain by taking a break from constant stimulation. Task: Go 12 hours without entertainment content today.

5. **Chapter 5: Phone Rules Setup**

    - Instead of abandoning your phone, set clear boundaries. Rules for phone usage will allow you to use it productively without falling into distractions.

      Task: Set rules like no phone in bed, fixed usage time, and no phone during study.

6. **Chapter 6: Trigger–Routine–Reward Loop**

    - Understanding the habit loop—how triggers lead to routines and rewards—will help you break the cycle of distractions.

      Task: Record the 3 biggest daily triggers that lead you to distraction.

7. **Chapter 7: Reflection Sunday**

    - It's important to pause and reflect on your progress, challenges, and growth. Reflection builds self-awareness, which is essential for further growth.

Task: Journal about what changed for you this week—what felt freeing, what was challenging.

Week 2: Building Focus Habits

8. Chapter 8: The 20-Minute Focus Sprint

- Focus works like a muscle. Start with small, focused sprints, such as 20-minute study sessions with breaks in between.

  Task: Do 1 focus sprint of 20 minutes of work, followed by a 5-minute break.

9. Chapter 9: Habit Anchoring

- Anchoring new habits to existing ones is an effective way to create consistency. For example, attach journaling to your morning routine.

  Task: Pick a daily habit (like brushing) to anchor your journaling.

10. Chapter 10: Morning Setup for Focus

- Your morning sets the tone for the rest of the day. Establish a phone-free morning routine to set yourself up for focused productivity.

  Task: Spend the first 30 minutes after waking up without your phone.

11. Chapter 11: Energy + Water + Food

- Low energy leads to low focus. Hydration and proper nutrition are crucial for maintaining focus throughout the day.

  Task: Track your water intake and avoid junk food for 24 hours.

12. Chapter 12: The Study Temple

- Your study space should be sacred, organized, and conducive to focus.

  Task: Declutter and decorate your study area to make it more inviting and productive.

13. Chapter 13: 1-Hour Study Ritual

- Your brain performs best when following rituals. Develop a 1-hour study ritual for productive study sessions.

  Task: Study for 60 minutes with full attention—note how it felt.

14. Chapter 14: Week 2 Review

- Reflect on the habits you've developed so far. Self-reflection is key to understanding your strengths and areas for improvement.

  Task: Write about what helped you focus the most this week and rate yourself out of 10.

Week 3: Mastering Your Mind and Control

15. Chapter 15: Thought Control 101

- You are not your thoughts. You are the master of them. Learn how to control negative or distracted thoughts and regain your focus

  Task: Write down 3 negative thoughts and how you can reframe them.

16. Chapter 16: Delay = Power

- Temptations weaken when you delay them. Try the 10-minute delay rule to break the instant gratification

cycle.
Task: Delay a distraction by 10 minutes before giving in.

17. Chapter 17: The 'Why' Wall

- Keeping your purpose in mind is powerful for resisting distractions. Create a "Why I Must Focus" poster to stay motivated.

  Task: Create a poster with reasons why you must focus and stick it on your wall.

18. Chapter 18: Boring is Powerful

- Don't fear boredom—it's where your brain regenerates. Sit in silence and embrace the boredom to improve your ability to focus.

  Task: Sit in silence for 10 minutes, no phone, no distractions.

19. Chapter 19: Declutter Your Mind

- Your mind is like a computer—it needs to clear the cache regularly. Writing down your thoughts will help declutter your brain.

  Task: Do a brain dump: write down everything on your mind for 10 minutes.

20. Chapter 20: Digital Minimalism

- Simplify your digital life by removing unnecessary apps and distractions.

  Task: Keep only 10 essential apps on your phone's home screen.

21. Chapter 21: Sunday Reflection

- Another reflection moment to assess your progress. Reflect on internal changes and share them with others.

  Task: Write about your biggest internal change so far.

Week 4: Maintaining Long-Term Focus

22. Chapter 22: The 5AM Rule (Even at 7AM)

- The key to a productive day starts early. Own your morning to ensure a more focused day.

  Task: Wake up and complete your first study session before 8AM.

23. Chapter 23: One Screen Rule

- Multitasking is a myth—focus on one screen at a time.

  Task: Use only one screen today and track your focus.

24. Chapter 24: Study With Me (Virtual Room)

- Studying in groups enhances focus. Join a study session for 45 minutes in a virtual group.

  Task: Join a silent study session via Zoom or YouTube.

25. Chapter 25: Reward Yourself Right

- Celebrate your victories by rewarding yourself for staying focused.

  Task: Plan a healthy reward for your efforts this week.

26. Chapter 26: Phone Lock Mode

- Lock your phone during specific periods to ensure distraction-free productivity.

  Task: Use Focus Mode or an app blocker from 6PM to 9PM today.

27. Chapter 27: 1% Daily Growth

- Focus isn't about giant leaps—it's about small, consistent progress.

  Task: Write down 3 micro-wins for the day.

28. Chapter 28: Focus for Life Blueprint

- The next 90 days are about long-term focus. Create a blueprint for maintaining focus beyond 30 days.

  Task: Create a 90-day Focus Plan.

29. Chapter 29: Your Final Test

- Test your focus by going distraction-free for 4 hours.
  Task: Go distraction-free for 4 hours today.

30. Chapter 30: Graduation Day: The Focused You

- Celebrate your transformation! You have completed the reset. Reflect on how far you've come, and lock in these focus habits for life.

Booster Chapter: Unlocking Financial Growth –

How to Build Millions

In the pursuit of focus and productivity, it's crucial to not only excel in the present but also to strategically plan and implement financial growth strategies. Whether you're looking to build a career or start a business, wealth creation requires a blend of mindset, discipline, and smart decision-making. Drawing inspiration from the top financial books, I've compiled the best practices and principles that will give you the tools you need to unlock millions in wealth. This chapter will guide you through the strategies that have made billionaires, entrepreneurs, and investors successful in building their financial empires.

1. The Millionaire Mindset – Think Big and Long-Term

The first step to financial success is to develop a millionaire mindset. As popularized by books like *Rich Dad Poor Dad* by Robert Kiyosaki and *Think and Grow Rich* by Napoleon Hill, the key to building wealth is thinking big and having a long-term vision.

- **Think Bigger:** Stop limiting your thoughts to small amounts of money. Think in terms of millions, not thousands. This mindset shift will allow you to set bigger goals and develop strategies to reach them. For example, instead of thinking, "I want to save $10,000 this year," think, "I want to create multiple streams of income that generate $1 million in five years."
- **Long-Term Vision**: Understand that wealth creation is a long game. Instant gratification can drain your resources. Prioritize long-term investments like stocks, real estate, or business ownership. Millionaires don't get rich overnight; they build wealth over decades.

2. Financial Literacy – Knowledge is Power

Many people work hard for money, but only those who understand how money works truly grow it. Books like *The Intelligent Investor* by Benjamin Graham and *The Millionaire Next Door* by Thomas Stanley emphasize the importance of financial literacy.

- **Learn the Basics of Investment:** Financial growth depends on understanding the difference between assets and liabilities. Build your asset base (stocks, real estate, businesses) while minimizing liabilities (debt, unnecessary expenses).
- **Investing Smartly:** Whether it's in the stock market, real estate, or starting your own business, make your money work for you. Learn about different investment vehicles like mutual funds, ETFs, real estate, and startups. Understand the risk and reward, and diversify your portfolio.
- **Avoid Financial Illiteracy:** A major mistake many people make is ignoring financial education.

Understanding compound interest, taxes, and debt management will give you the edge in wealth-building. Books like *The Simple Path to Wealth* by JL Collins or *Rich Dad's Guide to Investing* are invaluable resources.

3. The Power of Compound Interest – Let Time Work for You

In *The Compound Effect* by Darren Hardy and *The Richest Man in Babylon* by George S. Clason, the concept of compound interest is emphasized as one of the most powerful forces for wealth creation.

- **Start Early**: Compound interest grows exponentially. The earlier you start investing, the more time your money has to grow. Invest in growth assets, such as stocks or index funds, which can compound over time.
- **Consistency is Key:** Even small, consistent investments can lead to massive wealth over time. Make saving and investing a habit. Regularly contributing to investment funds or real estate properties can turn small amounts into millions in the long run.

4. Leverage – Using Other People's Money

In *The Rich Dad's Guide to Investing*, Kiyosaki talks about leveraging other people's money (OPM) as a means to accelerate wealth creation. Leverage allows you to amplify your returns without using your own capital.

- Business Leverage: Start a business that generates consistent cash flow. Use business loans or investor capital to fund your business ventures, rather than putting your own savings at risk. Be strategic in how you raise capital to scale your business rapidly.

- **Real Estate Leverage**: Real estate is one of the most powerful wealth-building tools. You can use mortgages to buy properties, allowing you to control valuable assets while only investing a small portion of your own capital. As the property appreciates, you reap the rewards of both capital gains and rental income.
- **Leverage Your Network:** Building relationships with mentors, partners, investors, and other entrepreneurs will give you access to resources, capital, and knowledge you might not otherwise have. Networking with successful people and learning from their experiences will save you time and money.

5. Networking and Building Relationships

According to books like *The Go-Giver* by Bob Burg and *How to Win Friends and Influence People* by Dale Carnegie, building strong relationships is one of the most crucial aspects of financial success.

- **Mentorship and Collaboration:** Surround yourself with successful individuals who can guide and challenge you. Find mentors who have built successful businesses or wealth. Learning from their experiences and mistakes can fast-track your own growth. Don't hesitate to collaborate with others to scale your ideas.
- **Creating Value for Others**: Successful wealth-builders create value for others before expecting rewards. The principle of value creation is fundamental. Build a business or an investment portfolio that solves problems for others, and the money will follow.

6. Business Ownership – Scale Through Entrepreneurship

If you want to generate millions, business ownership is a critical pathway. In books like *the E-Myth Revisited* by Michael E. Gerber and *Zero to One* by Peter Thiel, entrepreneurs are taught that scaling a business is one of the quickest ways to build wealth.

- **Build Scalable Businesses:** Focus on building businesses that are scalable. Start with a product or service that can be replicated or sold in large quantities. Whether it's a tech startup, a SaaS (Software as a Service) business, or a product-based business, focus on systems that allow growth without proportional increases in cost.
- **Automation and Delegation**: Focus on automating tasks that don't require your direct involvement. Hire and build teams that can take care of the operations while you focus on growth and strategic decision-making.

7. Take Calculated Risks

In *Principles* by Ray Dalio, the concept of taking calculated risks is highlighted as a crucial strategy for growing wealth. Wealth is rarely built without some level of risk.

- **Risk Management:** Understand the risks before you take them. Research thoroughly, be prepared for setbacks, and never invest more than you're willing to lose. However, don't be afraid to take risks that are calculated, well-researched, and within your control.
- **Start Small, Scale Fast**: When it comes to investments or starting a business, you can always start small and scale as you gain confidence and experience.

Test your ideas, see what works, and then double down on the successful models.

8. Mindset and Resilience

The most successful individuals, as shown in books like *Grit* by Angela Duckworth and *Atomic Habits* by James Clear, understand that perseverance and resilience are essential for long-term financial success.

- Overcome Failures: There will be setbacks along the way. Instead of being discouraged by failure, view it as an opportunity to learn and grow. Resilience is a key factor in making a fortune. Embrace challenges, learn from them, and keep pushing forward.
- Consistency and Discipline: Consistency is what separates the millionaires from the wannabes. Whether it's in investing, building your business, or networking, the most successful people make consistent efforts, day after day. This mindset of persistence leads to the accumulation of wealth over time.

Conclusion: The Millionaire's Blueprint

Building millions isn't about luck; it's about mastering financial principles, understanding how wealth is created, and using your time, resources, and efforts to build a legacy of wealth. Whether through investments, businesses, or leveraging the power of compounding, the strategies outlined in this chapter provide a blueprint for creating significant wealth.

By changing your mindset, improving your financial literacy, leveraging your resources, and building relationships, you can unlock your financial potential. The road to millions requires patience, discipline, and smart risk-taking, but by applying these strategies consistently, you will find yourself closer to your financial dreams.

Your journey to financial freedom and millions starts now. Keep learning, stay focused, and never stop growing.